INDIA'S GLORY

RAGHUPATI BHATT

Published in Australia
BIC Classification:
1FKA (Geographical: India), HBJQ (History),
HPDF (Philosophy), HRG (Hinduism)
978-0-9875598-6-9

NUMEN BOOKS
WWW.NUMENBOOKS.COM

INDIA'S GLORY

RAGHUPATI BHATT

BEFORE THE BOOK

SOME YEARS AGO I wrote a series of articles in the newspaper *Navhind Times* of Goa, India. They were published under the title "Glimpses of India's Glorious Past". I then thought of converting the set of articles into a book. Accordingly, I have edited the articles and added some additional data.

History is an interesting subject. If you forget history, you harm your present and future. Winston Churchill has said that forgetting history changes geography.

Many pages of India's history were rewritten after new information was unearthed. There was also an attempt to present biased history. The travellers who visited India have written a lot about India's history. The kings and emperors had their chroniclers who have noted down things. Our ancient kings inscribed the information. A lot of historical information came to light after the coins and copper plates were found. India has a rich literary tradition. We have picked up the things from literary texts too.

Many of the things mentioned in the following pages are not there in history books. The people who attempted to write down our history were mostly Europeans and they have written the history of India from their angle. For example, the British historians told us that the Queen of Jhansi did not want to fight with the British but she was forced into the mutiny. Godse Bhat's travel account says that he met the Queen in the jungle. She was on the run and she said to the author, "I am a widow. I would not have fallen into this but the love of this nation compelled me to get involved in this".

Similarly, nothing was known about Ashoka for a long time but after careful excavation and reading the inscriptions a very lucid picture emerged. Apart from the third party records, the great king himself has written a lot about himself which is not there in the text books.

The grains of truths have to be gleaned from different sources. The Portuguese records maligned the image of both Shivaji and his son Sambhaji. The records of the Mugals did the same. The whole history of the Marathas was written in a prejudiced way. Sometimes the translators got the meanings wrong. When Jadunath Sarcar's text was translated, it gave the impression that Sambhaji was in hiding and was drunk when he was caught by the Mugals.

I love my country and I think that she is wronged. In Pakistan they still write the wrong history. The land

which was part of India and which has a consistent history of many millennia was termed as barbarian and pagan (one of the earliest universities was established there and the first book of grammar was written in that part). The people from Pakistan are now giving the impression that the whole Indian subcontinent's history began after the Muslim Invasion.

This is an honest attempt to put down something in an unbiased way.

The observations in this book are based on the books I read. I have tried to crosscheck the information as much as possible.

I want to dedicate this book to the people of Peth Vadgaon in Kolhapur district; many of whom may not be able to read this book (some of them cannot read).

And I am indebted to you my readers forever.

RAGHUPATI BHATT

TABLE OF CONTENTS

SARE JAHANSE ACHCHA
HINDOSTAN HAMARA

THIS BOOK ATTEMPTS to talk about the golden ages of India's history objectively. These pages are about the period which Henry Derozio called "The Harp of India".

There are some wrong notions about India's history. One of them is that India was ruled by invaders for one thousand years or more. This is a blatant lie. The invaders ruled parts of India and they had been resisted all the time. Alexander, who boasted to be a world conqueror, was checked at the border of India. There were well established kingdoms in India. He could not even think of fighting with them. It would have ended him. The slave dynasty ruled over Delhi and there were well established kingdoms in the surrounding regions. Then the mighty Mugals came but they too had to struggle a lot and there were many kingdoms with whom they had to constantly fight. The same thing can be said about the British and the other colonial powers like the Portuguese. The British or the others had to fight incessantly and even then they could not rule peacefully.

The soul of India was never subdued. We have that fighting spirit. We have certain weaknesses which all other nationals have got. To say that India was always defeated is wrong. In fact the whole of India was never defeated. We cannot compare India with other countries because India is unique. Nowhere else in the world are so many people of different races living together. Nowhere else in the world, there are so many languages spoken. And there is no country in the world which has five thousand or more years of living civilization (China had one but they divorced their civilization).

When Iqbal wrote the lines, "*Sare Jahanse achcha Hindostan Hamara*", he had this India before him (even though he was a supporter of the Pakistan concept in later years). The concept of India encompasses even Pakistan, Afghanistan, Nepal, Myanmar, and Bhutan. '*Stan*' is a corrupt form of '*sthan*', a Sanskrit word signifies the larger India. Wherever this word has gone, India has gone. Ancient Persia and the culture there was the same as India. They worshipped the same gods we worshipped. It is argued by some that Native Americans like the Maya and the Inca were also Indians (literally, not in the sense that Columbus referred to them).

Mayasura, who was mentioned in one of the epic scriptures, was an excellent architect. He built wonderful accommodations for the kings. The word 'Maya' sounds like *Maya* and the Maya people of

America were known to be excellent architects. The word 'asur' is also found in the Assyrian culture. In far away Russia there are people who find languages similar to Dravidian languages.

India had overseas connections in the distant past. Indians did go abroad and had colonies, but not like the colonial powers of Europe. It was peaceful, without any bloodshed.

India has always had two sides, the good side and the bad side. The list of bad things is very long. Swami Vivekananda (an Indian monk) spoke highly about India when he toured Europe and America, but when he came back to India he criticized his brethren and praised the West.

He felt that India lacked the scientific attitude. He felt that Europeans were industrious people. He felt that India was unjust and cruel towards the backward caste people and also to women. He respected Islam for its equality.

It is written in history books that Robert Clive with a few men established his rule in India. The Indians could have fought with him but they didn't. His soldiers marched unobtrusively and people watched them with curiosity. Shivaji the Great fought many battles, but two thirds of them were against his own people. Rana Pratap had Muslims with him and the Mughals ran their empire with the help of Hindus. The Peshwas and their generals looted Mutts and temples whenever they were in need of money. Bajirao the First, whenever he was on any expedition, was not considerate about the crops. On the other hand Aurangzeb, the villainous tyrant wrote to his generals that they should not trouble the farmers and should not cause any harm to the crops. The sepoys of the Mutiny looted our own people because they were in need of money. They declared Bahadurshah Jaffar as the emperor of India but they were very contemptuous about him and they referred to him as "Budhha" which is a disrespectful addressing.

We have to accept certain things about us. We do not have the patriotism required to make India great. "*Mera Bharat Mahan*" is a mere slogan. We are not doing anything to make its meaning real.

But despite those things Iqbal was right in asserting that our country is better than all other countries in the world. Where do you find a mountain range like the Himalayas? Where do you find rivers like Ganga and Yamuna? There are no monsoon showers like India's anywhere. There are no deserts like India's deserts. You do not find people of such variety anywhere else as you find in India.

If you go to the Ghats of Kashi or Banaras, you can see traditions that go back up to four thousand years. The same Ganga, the same ghat, the same rituals and the same people who prayed there, died there. Time has stood still over there. I found the same thing in Udupi also. Udupi is an ancient town where there is a Shri Krishna Temple. If you go to the area where the temple is located, you will find that nothing has changed. It's the same as it was when the founder of the Dwaita (Dualism) cult Shri Madhvacharya started the practices. Even the lamps he lit are still burning.

Indian Muslims are Indians. They might be living in Pakistan or Bangladesh, but their basic identity is Indian. The same thing can be said about the Indian Christians. Buddhists, Jains, Sikhs and Lingayats and all the other religious sects of India have something very common in them. That is their Indianness. Nobody folds their hands in salutation as these people do.

Mother India can be seen in all these people and places and I salute her with the words "VANDE MATARAM".

LIFE AND TIMES OF
CHANDRAGUPTA MAURYA

CHANDRAGUPTA MAURYA WAS the first sovereign king after the times of the epics or the Classical age. Before him the Nandas ruled the Magadha Empire which had recorded history since epic times. The *Puranas* mention the Nandas and give details about the founder of the dynasty, Mahapadmananda. According to *Purana* traditions the Nandas were not Kshatriyas but were accepted as Kshatriyas.

There are doubts about Chandragupta's lineage but all scholars agree that he did not belong to the aristocracy. His mother was Mura so he was Maurya (of Mura). She perhaps worked in the palace as a maid servant. Some have wildly guessed that he was an illegitimate son of Dhanananda, whom he ousted.

Some Buddhist scholars think that he belonged to the clan of Maurya Kshatriyas of Pippalivana. Chandragupta's birth year is not known but his death took place around 300 B.C. The Jains have chronicled his times as in his later life he became a Jain.

Chandragupta spent his childhood in Taxila. This Taxila (also spelled as Taxshila) founded by king Taxa was a centre of learning. It had a famous university, whose masters were regarded as authorities in their subjects and were literally king makers. It was like the modern Harvard School of Business. The great Koutilya or Chanakya or Vishnugupta taught here. People from other parts of the world came here to study. The Chinese pilgrims made it their point to pay a visit to Taxila.

Chandragupta met Alexander the Great in Taxila. Perhaps he might have worked as a mercenary in Alexander's army. He also must have met his mentor and Guru, Arya Chanakya here. Legends say that he asked Alexander's help to oust Dhanananda. If he had, then he was committing the same mistake the later kings committed. But there is no proof of that story.

According to one legend Chanakya was insulted in the court of Dhanananda. He was made to get up which infuriated him. He took an oath that he would oust Nandas from power. Chanakya was a reputed scholar and he had trained many princes. He had so much self-confidence that he boasted he was able to make a king of anybody. Of course he needed the right material.

And he got it in Chandragupta. Chandragupta was playing with his friends and he was playing as a king. His gestures and body language impressed Chanakya. He knew that he was looking at the future emperor of India. He took Mura's permission and started training Chandragupta.

It could not be just these two. Most probably Dhanananda was also a tyrant. There was political unrest amongst the people and they were awaiting a savior.

The boy was trained in all affairs. Chandragupta himself was equally ambitious. Both of them needed each other. None was complete without the other. It was Chanakya who made Chandragupta join Alexander's army to find out its strengths and weaknesses. He was brought before Alexander. Alexander both liked and disliked his aggressive manners and attitude.

Then Chanakya and Chandragupta went on recruiting young men of caliber in their army. Their army grew slowly but surely. Still they were no match for the Magadha army. The Nandas were ruthless and immensely powerful so Chandragupta had to flee. It was a setback for Chandragupta and his Guru.

One day while both of them were passing a hut, they saw a woman serving rice to her son. The son got his fingers burnt because the rice was steaming hot. Then the mother said, "If you do like that fool Chandragupta, your fingers will get burnt. You have to take the rice from the sides which get cooled fast. Gradually you can move to the centre".

The illiterate woman taught Chandragupta the lesson. At the centre, the things are always hot. He went on attacking outer kingdoms and he became stronger. Finally Dhanananda's power was limited to Patliputra only and then it was easy to defeat him.

This ended the tyrannical rule of the Nandas. A new page opened; the rule of the Mauryas. Chanakya remained with Chandragupta for a good number of years. The rule of Chandragupta was peaceful and just. Chandragupta came to power in 321 B.C. when he was just twenty five years old.

Chanakya wanted to build a powerful kingdom. Under his guidance the Maurya Empire was built. The basic principles of Chanakya's policy are in the *Arthshastra* which is still regarded as the Bible of politics. The author is called Koutiliya because Chanakya was also known as Koutilya. There are some doubts about the authorship, but the authority of the book is never doubted. It goes on giving the duties of the king and his ministers, the rights of the citizens, the punishments for various crimes and also medicines for different ailments. The *Arthshastra* is also an important document which tells us about the times in which the book was written. It is also a compilation of the various 'isms' that were prevalent then.

According to one play "*Mudrarakshas*", Parvataka had a very efficient minister in his court who was called Rakshasa. He was loyal to his master King Parvataka but Chanakya made him join Chandragupta. In this way Chanakya brought many good people to Chandragupta's court who helped him to build his empire.

Chandragupta built an empire which lasted for a hundred years. His major achievement lies in the consolidation of small kingdoms that existed around Magadha. He defeated the Greeks. Alexander had gone back and had met his death on the way. He had given the charge to Selucus Niketar who had a hold in Punjab and Sindh. Chandragupta defeated Selucus and ended his empire. There is no description of the battle but there was a peace treaty. Selucus had to give his daughter in marriage to Chandragupta.

Plutarch says that Chandragupta ruled all over India. Punjab, Sindh, Gujarat and Kathiawad were under Chandragupta's rule. So from Himalaya to Mysore, from Malwa to the Arabian Sea, Chandragupta had his reign. He built this empire in a very short time span.

His sovereignty was accepted by the neighboring kingdoms and they had their ambassadors in his court.

The Greek ambassador to Chandragupta's court Megasthenes had kept an account of what he saw in Chandragupta's kingdom.

According to his accounts, people were happy under Chandragupta. Chandragupta had several ministers and innumerable officers who were all accountable to the king. His administrative service was very efficient. Five villages were looked after by one administrator called Gopa who had to report to one Rajuka who again had to report to Samahartru. Finally the reports reached the king. Every officer had to be very alert.

All the annexed states were administrated by governors who were mostly Chandragupta's sons.

Chandragupta collected taxes from the people and gave them excellent services in return. He had his own intelligence service in which he appointed prostitutes (*Arthashastra* has given importance to prostitutes who were called Ganikas and *Arthashastra* respects them as useful citizens). These Ganikas were treated as Govt. officers and were entitled to all the privileges of such officers.

Chandragupta is respectfully mentioned by Greek historians. Even though he had defeated them, he was not hostile towards them. The Jain writers also mention him. Their accounts might be exaggerated but there are grains of truth in them.

According to Jain sources, Chandragupta embraced Jainism and became an ascetic towards the end of his life. He was supposedly a disciple of Bhadrabhahu. Bhadrabhahu went to Shravanbelgol (where the tallest statue of Bahubali still exists). He did penance in that holy place. Chandragupta followed him and according to Jain sources he attained Kaivalya there.

There is a small hill there which is called Chandragiri, where according to Jain sources Chandragupta breathed his last. There is also one Jain Basti (a Jain shrine) which is named after Chandragupta. They say that Chandragupta did penance for twelve years and ended his life by Jain ascetic method (they give up food altogether and die).

Chandragupta's greatness lies in a number of things. According to Arnold Toynbee he unified India for the first time. He gave universal status to Indian culture. He was a people oriented ruler and ruled his country in a democratic way. His governance was ideal in many respects. He gave the people their right of representation. Accountability was very important for him. He himself was a Shaivite and later a Jain but he respected all faiths.

According to some historians Chandragupta filled the void after the Greeks left. But the fact that he gave stability and peace to the people of this country is a universally accepted fact.

EMPEROR ASHOKA:
PRACTICAL MINDED RULER

IN THE EARLIER times nobody knew much about Ashoka. The only thing that was known about him was he was Chandragupta Maurya's grandson. The scholars did not give much thought to him. The pillars that he had erected and which told a lot about him were buried deep in the earth. The locals called them by many other names like "Bhimki Laat" which meant it was a mace of Bhima the powerful Pandava warrior. After the inscriptions on the pillars were deciphered and a lot of material was gathered from the Buddhist texts from Sri Lanka, they came to know about the greatness of Ashoka. Ashoka himself was also responsible for the misunderstanding because sometimes he called himself "Piyadassi", "Devanam Piya", etc. A Sinhalise king called himself by that name, but later on it was discovered that the Sinhalise king was an admirer of Ashoka and they had met each other. Only then a powerful and clear picture of Emperor Ashoka emerged.

Ashoka was the first king to inscribe in local scripts. Ashoka's empire was bigger than the earlier kings because the rock pillars called Askokastambha are found everywhere. His inscriptions are in Brahmi and Kharosti scripts. How the scholars deciphered the scripts and rewrote the history of one of the greatest kings of all times, is itself the content of a best seller.

Ashoka's pillars, some standing, some buried and some lying in a dilapidated state are found all over South East Asia. In addition to these inscriptions, Devanam piya or Piyadassi was mentioned in the record of Buddhist monasteries in Sri Lanka. It was established that they were referring to one and the same person. This was in the year 1905. The Sri Lankan records talked about Piyadassi (the Prakrit of Priyadarshi meaning 'one who is dear to look at'), who had baffled the scholars, but the inscriptions confirmed that he was Ashoka.

Ashoka came to power in 273 B.C. after the death of his father Bindusara. Bindusara had many sons from his many wives. Ashoka had rough skin, and because of that he had some problems. He was not good to look at; a man of short stature and perhaps with a pot belly. Ashoka was working as a governor when the news of his father's death came. Ashoka rushed back and killed all other claimants to the throne and assumed power.

According to legends there were many phases in the life of Ashoka. At one phase he was a lusty man (which he remained to the end of his life, because in all the depictions of Ashoka he is surrounded by voluptuous women), because of which he was called Kamashoka. Then when he assumed power, he became so ruthless that he was called Chandashoka.

His father Bindusara was an insignificant man. There are no achievements to his credit. He was Chandragupta's son and Chandragupta had given a lot to him in legacy.

But Ashoka was different. He was ambitious and cunning. It is said that his father was not happy with him. Or perhaps the other wives of the king had deliberately kept him away from the capital.

Regardless of that, he was very ambitious and he wanted to expand the Maurya Empire. Almost all the small kingdoms had accepted the authority of the Mauryas and they were feudal states now. But the Kalinga people had not accepted their sovereignty. Ashoka did not like that. When every attempt to conquer Kalinga was thwarted by the Kalinga people (Kalinga is modern day Orissa or Odessa), he invaded Kalinga with a huge army.

This battle changed the life of Ashoka. Kalinga was overpowered but at the cost of many lives. There were corpses on the ground. The widows were weeping, the children were distraught. The vultures were hovering over the battleground. It was a feast for them. It was a bloody sight. When Ashoka saw this he was moved from within. The violence, the mourning, and the bloody mess had a deep impact on his mind. He decided to purge violence from his life.

Ashoka became a Buddhist. He wore a long robe. He lived in his palace totally detached from worldly things. Ashoka followed the guidelines given by Buddha. A Buddhist has to live like a Bhikku.

But Ashoka lived two lives. He was outwardly a Bhikku but he never forgot that he was a king. Even though he was a Buddhist, he maintained his army. He might not have made any acts of aggression afterwards but he knew that he had to maintain his empire.

He was active in Buddhist movements. A Buddhist conference was organized in his times. It is believed that he might have played an active role in the organization. He then thought of spreading Buddhism in the world. He had manpower and he used it to the fullest. According to Sri Lankan records he sent his son Mahendra and daughter Sanghmitra to Sri Lanka.

He erected pillars all over his empire and wrote inscriptions on them. He defined Dhamma to the wandering monks. He gave them directions on what was to be done and what was to be avoided by the Bhikkus. His inscriptions were in local language so that everbody could understand them. He was definitely ahead of his times. What he wrote in those days is applicable even to this day. Here is an example.

"Sympathy for the servants, obedience to the parents, generosity for the priests and Bhikkus... but Devanam priya does not give importance to prestigious gifts but regards the fundamental development of all faiths as very important. The base for this control over one's speech in order not to praise one's faith more or run down other faiths…one who respects other faiths commands respect for his own faith and increases the impact of his own faith. If acted otherwise, he causes a great loss to his faith…so listen to what other faiths have to say."

Ashoka not only preached, he practiced what he preached. He gave alms to the priests, who practiced Brahminism, Jainism, or Buddhism. Of course he was more liberal towards the Bhikkus.

In one picture on a stupa, he looks ill and is supported by his wife. One reason might be that his sons were fighting for the throne. His favorite son was blinded by the rival queens.

Ashoka ruled for 37 years. His rule was peaceful. He governed justly and Buddhism reached the far corners of the world because of his efforts. This is one example of what he has written about himself.

"I have planted trees by the side of the road so that the animals and the travelers can get some shed to rest. After every nine miles I have arranged mango parks, wells and rest houses. There are drinking water tanks for people and animals. This was done by many other kings in the past but I have done it so that people may abide by the Dhamma."

Ashoka died around 237 B.C. He might have died a sad man because his sons had become restless by then. He wanted to give something to the Sangha which he did every year but he had nothing but a bhikshapatra with him.

There was a non-Buddhist faction who was preparing to revolt. One of Ashoka's queens was leading them. The blinding of Kunala (his favorite son) might have been a part of the conspiracy.

The sick emperor wanted to donate a large sum to his favorite Sangha which was vehemently opposed by the council of ministers. Prince Samprati ordered that nothing should be given to the Sangha.

The Chinese traveler Xuanzang has given the description. According to him the ailing king wanted to give all his valuables to the Sangha but his ministers would not allow him.

Ashoka is depicted in Amravati stupa as a wheel turning monarch. That is "Chakravarti" in Sanskrit. He was religious as well as practical. He adhered to dharma but never forgot that dharma alone cannot sustain the empire. Like the King Janaka he was a Rajarishi. He evolved from Chandashoka to Kamashoka and finally to Dhammashoka. He called himself a Devanam Piya when Buddhism rejected the concept of God. It shows the practical side of Ashoka. He was an emperor of the people who were religious and for whom the existence of God was very essential.

SAMUDRAGUPTA & VIKRAMADITYA: THE LEGENDARY KINGS

THE MAURYAN EMPIRE did not last long after Ashoka. In the last days of Ashoka, the Brahminism back-fired. The last Maurya emperor was assassinated while he was observing the parade. His name was Bruhadratha. That ended the Maurya rule. The leader of this revolt was his general Pushyamitra Shunga, who was a Brahmin and who founded the Shunga dynasty. According to historians there were many Maurya kings afterwards but they had small kingdoms. The seat of power was with the Shungas. Pushyamitra's son Agnimitra became the protagonist of the play *"Malvikagnimitram"*. In Pushyamitra's times Kalinga again became powerful under Kharvela.

The next great dynasty was that of the Gupta's. There were many Guptas before but they were either generals or petty kings. The first sovereign was Chandragupta I. He strengthened himself by marrying a Lichchavi princess. He tried to annex the neighboring kingdoms to Magadha.

Chandragupta I was followed by his son Samudragupta. He was also known as "Kacha". Samudragupta was chosen by his father as the worthiest among his sons. This event might have taken place around 325 A.D.

Samudragupta aimed to annex all the small kingdoms. He wanted to be the king of kings, the Samrat or Chakravarti. And he did conquer all the northern states and appointed governors. He also came down to the south, but in the south he just made them accept his authority. He defeated them but did not annex their kingdoms.

It is said that Kalidas' "*Raghuvansham*" is actually describing Samudragupta's conquests in the guise of Raghu's conquests. Samudragupta was indeed a great warrior, and a good king. Even though he was a Vaishnava, he did not interfere in the religious matters of the people. A Chinese traveler has written that the king of Sri Lanka had sent an emissary to seek permission from Samudragupta to build a monastery at Bodh Gaya. Samudragupta allowed him.

Samudragupta also performed the Ashwamedha. In the Ashwamedha, a horse is led through many countries. If the horse is stopped, there is a war between the defender of the horse and the detainer of the horse. Afterwards the horse is sacrificed. Many kings performed this ritual but only issued coins bearing the letters 'Ashwamedha'.

Samudragupta was a man of many talents. According to one account he could play many musical instruments. This is also supported by coins which show him playing some instruments. He also wrote some musical compositions.

He was also a poet and had composed some great poetic works. None of his works survived. Perhaps they perished with him otherwise the later poets would have mentioned them.

Raychoudhuri has compared him to Ashoka. He says that despite the difference, these two great men had many things in common. Both insisted on Dharma (not in the sense of religion, but Dharma as duties). Ashoka was violent in the beginning but later he became very tolerant. Both of them made wars but both of them were very lenient or understanding to their enemies. Both of them had big empires and they loved their subjects.

Samudragupta chose Chandragupta II as his successor. According to many scholars Chandragupta II was the legendary Vikramaditya. In course of time, people realized that they couldn't have a better king. Chandragupta II was a valiant king; he controlled a big empire and was the object of legends in his lifetime.

Vikramiditya's accession was around 381 A.D. He ruled until 413 A.D. Chandragupta II married a princess of the Naga dynasty. The Nagas had their kingdoms in the border states so this was a political alliance.

Chandragupta II or Vikramaditya was ambitious. According to one inscription, he wanted to conquer the whole world, especially the Shaka strongholds. That was why he became known as 'Shakari' or one who vanquished the Shakas. Vikramaditya had his capital in Patliputra in the beginning. Later he shifted to Vidisha and finally settled in Ujjain.

Dr. Bhandarkar concludes that Chandragupta II was Vikramaditya as the words 'Vikram sinha' and 'Vikramaditya', are inscribed on many of his coins.

The legends about Vikramaditya are in *Vetal Panchvishi* (twenty five stories about Vetala or the ghost) and *Sinhasan Battishi* (thirty two stories about the royal throne).

According to a play written about Vikramaditya, Ramgupta ascended the throne after Samudragupta. He was a weakling. As soon as he came to power the Shakas invaded. Samudragupta was dead and Ramgupta was weak so they wanted to take advantage. Ramgupta was defeated and to further humiliate him he was told to send his wife to the Shaka general. Ramgupta agreed. The Gupta subjects were shocked to learn about this humiliation.

Chandragupta II went to the Shaka camp in the guise of Dhruvadevi, the wife of Ramgupta. He was a daredevil. He killed the Shakas and came back victorious.

This act of Chandragupta made him the beloved of the people. He became an icon. Ramgupta envied his valor and tried to kill him deceptively but all his attempts failed and finally he himself got killed. Later

Vikrama married Dhruvadevi and ascended the throne. This story is supported by the coins of Ramgupta and Vikramaditya. This play titled "*Devichandraguptam*" is perhaps based on historical facts.

He ascended the throne in the year 381 A.D. Vikram samvat was started to commemorate this event. So Chandragupta II assumed the name Vikramaditya. Vikrama means valor and Aditya means sun.

One of Vikramaditya's daughters was married into the Vakataka family. Another daughter was married in the royal house of Vidarbha. After her husband's death, this daughter Prabhavati ruled Vidarbha. Because of these marriage relations Chandragupta II had a large empire.

Vikramaditya loved poetry and other forms of arts. He was a patron to many artists. He also might have contributed to the world of literature (it may have been lost in the course of time). According to one inscription he had appeared for a Sanskrit test.

The great poet Kalidasa was in his employment. In Kalidasa's plays Ujjain appears many a times. Vikrama must have sent him on diplomatic missions. He was sent to Vidarbha (where Vikrama's daughter lived), to Kolhapur and to Kuntalesh. Kalidasa has also written a play titled "*Vikramorvashiyam*" which is a love tale woven around the King and the celestial dancer Urvashi.

Vikrama was a Vaishnavite but he patronized all religions (all Gupta kings were like him). He was a very caring king who valued the happiness of his subjects

above all. His support to literature and men of letters made him popular with that class which is why there is a lot of literature which revolves around Vikramaditya.

The scholars are not sure whether he started Vikram Samvat or not. There were many kings who called themselves Vikramaditya. But the word Shakari fits him. He had defeated the Shakas. Vikrama in the tales is perhaps a fictitious creation but is definitely modeled on this Vikramaditya. Some of his exploits appear in these tales.

According to one story given to us by Sir Richard Burton, there was one Gardabhsena (literal meaning donkey). He got married to a princess.

The son born to them was Vikrama. There are many folk tales about him. In Marathi there is a play based on this legend called *"Gadhavache Lagna"* meaning the marriage of a donkey.

As there are many stories about him, Vikramaditya must have been a good king and an ideal ruler.

Vikramaditya lived in Ujjain. Ujjain has many stories about him. There is a Vikrama temple there and inside there is a life size statue of Vikramaditya. It is said that the earlier statue had been of pure gold.

HARSHAVARDHANA

&

PULAKESHI II

AFTER VIKRAMADITYA (CHANDRAGUPTA II), his son Kumargupta came to power. His reign was peaceful but he had to fight with the Huns very often. The decline of the Guptas began in Kumargupta's times. After Kumargupta, his son Skandgupta also had to deal with the Huns. The influx was unstoppable. The Huns were swarming in. Additionally, he had to fight the insurgents too.

After Skandgupta, the Gupta Empire started to disintegrate. Many of the branches of the Gupta dynasty declared independence and started ruling from different places. Each branch started calling itself as the main branch. Chaos ruled everywhere.

During these troubled times one king tried to give stability to India by annexing the small kingdoms and establishing a reign of peace.

This king was Harshavardhana (Harsha means joy

and vardhana means growth). Harsha ruled during the seventh century. He was the son of Prabhakarvardhana. There are records of Harsha because he had Banhbhatta in his court who has written his biography. This biography is titled *Harshacharitam*. Banhbhatta was a man of letters who was known for his signature work called *Kadambari*.

India had no central power during Harsha's reign. There were many small states. They were independent and were always battling with each other. Among these states, Prabhakarvardhana's Thaneshwar was the strongest. He was requested to bring all the small states together.

Harsha came to power after his father's death. He was a peace-loving and caring ruler. He liked to be in contact with the people to find out their difficulties.

Every year he gave alms to the people. There are pictures of him with his sister Rajshri, who was a widow. After her husband's death she lived with her loving brother. Both of them are shown as giving alms to the poor. Every year he distributed whatever he had to the poor till nothing was left with him.

Harsha annexed all the small states and ruled over a vast kingdom in the north. He could have come to the south also but another powerful king from the south Pulakeshi II of the Chalukya dynasty, defeated him and Harsha had to retreat. The Vindhya mountain range was the boundary for Harsha's empire and he had to be content with that.

Harsha was happy with that. He never came to the south but ruled major parts of the northern country. He was a patron of arts and culture. He liked to have religious discussions with monks. He had also sent his envoy to China. The famous Chinese traveler and scholar Huen Tsang came to India during his times. From Huen Tsang's writing it is clear that people were happy during Harsha's times. Harsha himself was a reputed scholar who wrote commentaries on religious works (as told by Banhbhatta).

Huen Tsang had come to study Buddhist scriptures in their original form. He stayed at Nalanda University and had discussions with the Acharyas (the professors in the university). Harsha had sent a message that he wanted to meet the Chinese scholar; the feudal king who patroned Huen Tsang was annoyed with the summons. The king was no match for Harsha but it was a question of honour. But Huen Tsung avoided the confrontation. He himself expressed the wish that he wanted to meet Harsha.

Huen Tsang met Harsha and was happy after the meeting. He found the king intelligent and well read. He noted that the king liked the company of scholars.

In one of the Gandhar paintings Harsha is shown giving away everything he had and finally asking his sister to give him a cloth to cover himself. Harsha would have ruled the whole of India if not for Pulakeshi II.

Pulkeshi was a Chalukya king and a warlord. He was also a lover of art and culture. He was Shaivite but respected all religions. The beautifully carved cave temples came into existence during the Chalukya times. The Chalukyas were happy in the south and their capital was Badami.

A mural of Pulkeshi II exists, but there is not much information about Pulakeshi. Harsha had Banbhatta and Huen Tsang while Pulakeshi had nothing. But these two were contemporaries and were equally great.

PRITHVIRAJ CHAUHAN

THERE IS A long poem based on the life of Prithviraj Chauhan. It is titled "Prithviraj Raso". Supposedly this was written by his friend "Chandvardai" who was a constant companion to this warrior.

Prithviraj was a Rajput King. He belonged to the Chauhan clan. The Rajputs emerged in the ninth century. There is no fixed opinion about their origin. According to some they were the Huns, who got mixed into the Hindu culture and claimed the status of Kshatriyas. Another legend says that the four clans of the Rajputs: Pratihar, Chauhan, Solanki and Parmar sprang up from a warrior, who was born of the Agnikunda (which means fire). Anyway, the word Rajput has come from the Sanskrit Rajputra meaning the prince. Even their clan names are corrupt forms of Sanskrit words. For example the word 'Solanki' comes from Chalukya.

The Rajputs do have some of the qualities of Huns in them. They were valiant and they had the same ruthlessness but then Rajputs had some qualities which the Huns did not have. They might have developed them in the course of Hinduisation.

The Brahmins gave them the status of Kshatriyas. They were always fighting with each other. The Brahmins or another class who were called the Bhat and Charan wove stories around them and gave them the lineage they wanted.

So some of them were Suryavanshi and some of them were Chandravanshis. Suryavansha is the Sun's clan so they could trace their ancestry to Rama. Chandravansha is the Moon's clan to which the famous Kauravas and Pandavas belonged.

Sometimes they came together to fight the aggressions. There are many of these wars in history and Prithviraj stands the tallest among them. It was Anangpal Tomar who came to Delhi to rule. Tomars ruled this part of India. According to legends he had a divine call to establish his kingdom where the Pandavas ruled. Anangpal built the oldest part of Delhi called the Surajkund.

Prithviraj took over from Anangpal. He was a seasoned warrior and a good king and was very popular with the other small kings. Prithviraj had built Lal Kot in Delhi. Delhi still has some monuments of Prithviraj. In local language he is called "Pithora".

There was enmity between Prithviraj and his cousin Jaychand Rathod who was a king of neighbouring Kanouj. He had a beautiful daughter whose name was

Samyukta or Samyogita. She loved Prithviraj. Jaychand did not like Prithviraj at all. He took every opportunity to run down Prithviraj.

Jaychanda arranged a swayamvara for Samyukta. In this the princes from different kingdoms are invited and they are introduced to the host princess. Each prince is described with his qualities and achievements. Finally the princess decides and chooses one who is most fit for her.

Prithviraj was not invited. To run him down Prithviraj's statue was placed at the door as a doorkeeper. That was Jaychand's way of running Prithviraj down.

But poor Jaychand didn't know that it was the idea of Prithviraj's group.

Samyukta wanted Prithviraj to come. She had sent him an invitation. Rajputs don't go anywhere uninvited. Samukta came with the garland for the swayamvara and the statue of Prithviraj came alive. It was Prithviraj himself standing like a statue. He literally lifted Samyukta and ran away to his kingdom.

This was something that Jaychand could not take lightly. The man whom he loathed had taken away his daughter. His daughter loved him but he was not ready to accept that fact. He wanted to finish off Prithviraj. Prithviraj was a seasoned warrior. None could beat him in arm to arm combat. His army was powerful. It was undefeated.

In anger, Jaychand made a mistake which changed the course of history.

He invited Muhammad Ghori of Ghur. Ghori had heard about India's wealth and he was waiting for an opportunity to plunder India. This was a godsend to him. He came to India with a huge army.

The armies of Prithviraj and Ghori met at Tarai. Prithviraj had called his friends. The Rajputs were seasoned warriors. Ghori was defeated and caught but Prithviraj pardoned him. It was the Rajput way. If anybody surrendered he was not to be punished.

Ghori did not forget and did not forgive. He studied the habits of Rajputs. He came to know about their weaknesses. With a huge army he struck again at the right moment. He was determined and strong. The Rajputs were off guard.

They were unprepared and were under the impression that they had taught Ghori a lesson and he would not strike again. The Rajputs were defeated and Prithviraj was killed in the fierce battle.

Prithviraj Raso gives another story. According to that Prithviraj fought valiantly but he was caught by Ghori's men. Ghori took him to his capital where Prithviraj was tortured.

The Rajputs were able to check the invaders for five hundred years. Their bravery and war techniques were superb but they lacked the cunning required.

They gave undue importance to their so-called virtues and always fought with each other on minor issues when unity was the need of the hour. Like the Huns they fought head strong without giving any thought to their safety and they lacked foresight. One has to retreat sometimes to gain time which was against their character.

According to Raso, Prithviraj's spirit was indefeatible to the end. In the end he was blinded. His friend Chandvaradai was witness to Prithviraj's courage. Finally he was to be executed in an arena in front of thousands of spectators.

Prithviraj was asked his last wish. He asked for a bow and an arrow. As he was blind nobody took his wish seriously. Chandvaradai knew that Prithviraj was Shabdavedhi. He could shoot following the sound.

When Prithviraj prepared to shoot he did not know where Ghori sat. But the generous Rajput had heard an exclamation of surprise from Ghori. Following the sounds, Prithviraj shot him. Ghori died instantly.

Later Prithviraj was also killed but he had taken his revenge. Prithviraj Raso tells us that Prithviraj had defeated and captured Ghori twice and twice he was let go by the generous Rajput which cost him his life in the end. Ghori did not reciprocate that generosity.

This story is not supported by history books. They say that Prithviraj met his death on the battleground

But Afgahan tradition backs Prithviraj Raso. A few years back there was an article in the Indian newspaper *Indian Express* written by a former diplomat. He was shown a place where Ghori was buried. This tomb was underground. To go to Ghori's tomb, he had to step compulsorily on a stone. He was told that under that stone the mortal remains of Prithviraj Chauhan were buried. This means that only after stepping on Prithviraj could you see the tomb of Ghori. This hatred was kept alive for many centuries and backs the story that Prithviraj killed Ghori in his den.

And there lies the glory of our great king Prithviraj who has remained alive in folklore. It is argued by some people that the famous Kutub Minar was started by either Prithviraj or his uncle Vigraharaj.

According to Raziuddin Aquil Raja, Prithviraj was cursed by the Sufi saint Muin-ud-Din Chishti of Ajmer. This saint had come to Ajmer because in a dream the Prophet himself had told him to go to India. When Muin-ud Din reached Ajmer, Raja Pithaura was the king.

The king and his men did not like the presence of the Sheikh there so the Sheikh and his disciples were harassed. But the Sheikh had miraculous powers so they could not do anything. Later one of the disciples was treated in a very bad way. The Sheikh sent word but Pithaura refused to accept it. Then the Sheikh said,

"*Pithaura ra zinda giraftim wa dadim ba lashkara ba Islam.*" (Prithviraj has been captured alive and handed over to the army of Islam).

Even this story from the Sufi records backs Prithviraj Raso.[1]

[1] RAZIUDDIN AQUIL, *In the Name of Allah* (New Delhi, Penguin

GOUTAMA, THE BUDDHA

OUTAMA, THE BUDDHA, was one person who was born some three thousand years ago and who conquered the world without using any arms. He was born a prince and he could have become a great king or perhaps a world conqueror like Alexander.

He was born in the year bordering 563 B.C., either in India or Nepal. According to some he was born in Uttar Pradesh, India. Lumbini, which is in Nepal bordering Uttar Pradesh, is also regarded as the birthplace of this great man. Uttar Pradesh Govt. identifies a location on their tourist map as the birth place of Gautama, the Buddha. Gautama lived a long life of eighty years and most of his life was spent in India. He might have been born in Lumbini, Nepal, but he attained Buddhahood in India. He gave his first sermon in India and the faith that is called Buddhism was Indian.

He had many names. He was given the name Siddhartha by his father. He was called Gautam because he was reared by his aunt whose name was Gautami. He was called Buddha because he had that wisdom with him. He is also known as Shakyamuni because he belonged to the clan of the Shakas or the Scythians. He was also called Tathagata.

The Scythians were barbarians when they came to India. The Guptas had a tough time fighting with them. But by Buddha's times they were Hinduised and were given the rank of Kshatriyas.

The Scythians had Gantantras or democratic states. Gautama's father Shuddhodhan belonged to the Lichchavi clan. This clan was powerful and every central power in India had to take congnizance of them. His mother was Mayavati or Mayadevi. She had strange dreams when she was pregnant. She saw a white elephant. The astrologers told the king that a very unusual child would be born to them (this scene is depicted on a rock at Lumbini which is supposedly the birthplace of Gautama).

In the course of time the child was born. The healthy boy had all the best qualities in him. The epic hero Rama was regarded as a perfect man with thirty two qualities in him. This was another such child born in Lichchavi clan which was already linked with Suryavansha, Rama's clan. His mother died soon after his birth.

The boy Siddhartha was taken care of by his aunt Gautami who gave the name Gautama to him.

The astrologers predicted that the child would either become a world conqueror or he may renounce the world to become a monk. The king was worried, because he wanted Gautama to become a world conqueror. The king gave orders that there should not be anything near Gautama which would make him sad.

So a beautiful palace was built for him surrounding which there was a garden with beautiful flowers that bloomed twelve months of the year. Young and beautiful women were appointed to be at the beck and call of Gautama. In short it was seen that he would see only the lovely things in life and there was no sadness or grief nearby.

There are stories of Gautama's cousin Devadatta who did not like Gautama. One reason might be that Gautama was to be the future king. Another reason might be Gautama had all the qualities of a perfect man which Devadatta lacked. Shuddodhan also had him married to Yashodhara, a princess. In the course of time a son was born to the couple who was named Rahul. Everything was good, better or the best in Gautama's life. There was no place for ugly, sad or old in Gautama's life. His father had taken great pains for that. Gautama was very happy with his happy family.

Despite all the efforts, Gautama saw the things he was not supposed to see. One day, when he was weary of the things he saw everyday, he told his charioteer to take him out. When they were on the road, Gautama saw a beggar, a sick man, then an old man, and finally a corpse. The charioteer told him that it was the destiny of every one who was born. Nobody can escape that.

Gautama became very disturbed. He now knew that the world created around him was superficial. The real world was full of misery. He was told that one who is born is sure to suffer from sickness, old age, turn of fortune, and finally death. Gautama wanted to find out why these miseries come and whether there was any remedy for them.

That decided the course of life for Gautama. He left his home, the luxuries, his sleeping wife and child, and proceeded for penance. He knew that if they were awakened, he would not be allowed to leave. It was very painful to leave those near and dear ones. His father would have done his utmost to stop him so he left at the dead of night.

For many years he was wandering through cities, villages, and forests. That was his penance. He saw the miseries of people and it made him sad and determined. After six years of wandering through life, one day when he was sitting under a peeple tree, the enlightenment came to him. This happened at Gaya, a very holy place for the Hindus. The tree under which he was enlightened came to be known as Bodhivriksha. A temple was erected at the place later, which is today the Mahabodhi temple. Ironically this tree was vandalized by one of the queens of Ashoka, who was responsible for the spread of Buddhism in the world.

Now Gautama became known as "Buddha" or the enlightened one. The day was Buddha Pournima. According to Shri Aurobindo, Buddha could have attained Nirvana on that day but he thought to himself, "How can I think of liberating myself when millions of my brethren are rotting in misery?" Buddha started teaching what he had realized. He gave four truths to the people.

His first truth was life is full of suffering. The second truth was that all the suffering arises because of desires and attachments. The third truth was if we give away desires and attachments, we can end our suffering. Fourthly one must have righteous behavior and attitudes towards all living beings.

This fourth truth implied that there should not be violence. Gautama the Buddha was the first one to think about all living beings compassionately. Buddha talked against violence. Buddha also rejected the concept of God. He felt that there was something called "Asat" beyond this world. He was sure that the non-attached, desireless, non-violent righteous beings who are compassionate to all living beings, get merged in this Asat which is called Nirvana.

Buddha took many things from Hinduism which was in the hands of Brahmins then and is called Brahminism by many scholars. As he denied the existence of God, he was also against rituals like Yadnya, sacrifice, and also the priestly class.

According to one theory Buddha was the need of the hour. The ritualistic religion was exploiting the people. There was excess of everything. Some messiah was needed to rescue the people and Buddha became a savior.

Buddha gave his first sermon at a place called Sarnath, which is near Kashi, the holiest place for

Hindus. Then most probably Buddha must have toured all over India. There were some kings like Prasenjeet (Pasenadi in Buddhist records) who were of Buddha's age, and according to the Buddhist texts were Buddha's friends.

Buddha used the common man's language and talked with the people in their language. He was against caste discrimination. Buddha's door was open for all. People from higher castes as well as the untouchables were welcomed with open arms. One became a Bhikku after entering the Sangha or the commune.

Buddha did not allow women in the Sangha in the beginning, but afterwards he had to give in because of his aunt Gautami. Gautama talked to the people about the miseries of life and how one could get rid of them. He denied the existence of God but insisted on right behavior and right attitude. His ideas were revolutionary but not foreign. He had taken some ideas from the Hindu scriptures. The concept of Karma was already there. The foreign scholars now refer to it as a Buddhist principle.

The Charvaka school of thought had always denied the existence of God. What was new was Buddha's compassion. He talked in parables like Jesus, five hundred years before him. He talked against the priestly class who acted as middlemen between God and man. He might not have been against the caste system but he treated all as one.

There are a number of legends about Gautama. All of them may not be true, but the essence of them is that Gautama was immensely popular with the common people. His denial of rituals might have given a relief to the people who were fed up with such things. Everyday he taught to thousands of disciples. Once Ajatshatru, the popular king and son of Bimbisara, came to seek his advice. He was surprised to see thousands of people listening to Buddha in pin drop silence.

There is also a story of Angulimala who was a dacoit, and who cut and stored the thumbs of his victims. He met Buddha, whom was not at all scared of him. There was a transformation and Angulimala gave up his bad ways and became a Bhikku.

Gautama lived a long life. He died at the age of eighty. Ironically this prophet of non-violence died of food poisoning because of the meat he had eaten at a disciple's place.

Buddha did not want to establish any new religion. He just wanted the people to live in a harmonized way. To live and let live was his advocacy. He had the support of the kings (it can be said that the phenomenon of the Buddha was a Kshatriya answer to the Brahmin class).

Buddhism spread to the far corners of India. There were monasteries established all over. They were called viharas. In the times of Ashoka, a few centuries later, in Magadha there were so many vihars that Magadha itself earned the name Vihar, which later became Bihar.

Buddha was defeated by his disciples. One who did not believe in God was made a God. Buddhism had many factions afterwards. Mahayana and Hinyana were the two major ones. Then there are Therwada, and Shinto, etc. Buddhism reached China and the thinkers like Lao-Tse and his Taoism, Confucious and his 'ism' etc., all got merged into Buddhism.

The *Jataka Tales* talk about the previous incarnations of Buddha as Bodhisatwa. It is an interesting document about the earlier days of Buddhism. Whatever was not desired by Buddha entered Buddhism after Buddha. Tibetan Buddhism is full of rituals.

At one time Buddhism was spread throughout India. We find the relics of viharas and Buddhist caves all over India, but after the Gupta age and Shankracharya's victory over Buddhism, Buddhism literally disappeared from India. Even though it was spread all over the world, it was after Babasaheb Ambedkar's embracing Buddhism that Buddhism gained a good following. Millons of Ambedekar's followers also entered Buddhism.

Recently the Taliban destroyed huge statues of Buddha in Damiyan in Afghanistan. It is proof that Buddha is sill powerful.

VARDHAMAN MAHAVEER:
THE REORGANIZER OF JAINISM

VARDHAMANA MAHAVEERA, THE twenty fourth Thirthankara of the Jains was a contemporary of Buddha. According to the Jain traditions he was the guru of Buddha. Both of them were princes, and both of them had renounced their near and dear ones. Both of them were Kshatriyas and both of them were social reformers. It is possible that they might have met. They might have been admirers of each other. According to the Jains, Adinatha was the first (adi means beginning), and the last was Mahaveera.

Mahaveera's life span was from 540 to 468 B.C. He was born in the royal family of Magadha. He belonged to the Lichchavi Clan which was very powerful. He gave up his life of luxuries and became an ascetic at the age of thirty.

Like Buddha, he too wandered in the forest and did penance. He followed "Nirgranthas" a sect founded by Parshwanatha. The monks in this order do not follow any book.

Granthas are books and nir denotes negation. The monks move naked. They are totally unattached to anything. All Tirthankaras followed this method.

Mahaaveera underwent many hardships. He gave a lot of pain to his body. He went without food for several days. He became emaciated. Once while he was sitting a under a tree, a man came and in order to make Mahaveera angry, took a sharp stick and pierced Mahaveera's ear. Mahaveera was bleeding but he did not say a word to that fellow. Finally that fellow was ashamed of himself.

Mahaveera was called Jina after attaining knowledge which literally means a conqueror. He had conquered his sense organs by giving hardship to them. This was the ancient way of the Tirthankaras who were also called Jinas. Mahaveera organized the ancient sect and his followers are called Jains (Very recently the Govt. of India recognized them as a minority community).

Jainism does not believe in God; it is an atheistic religion. They do not follow any books. The followers of Mahaveera converted him and the previous Tithankaras into gods. The temples were erected and idol worship followed.

The word Mahaveera also means a great warrior. In the Hindu pantheon of gods, Hanuman who was a great warrior, is also called Mahaveera. Mahaveera fought a great battle with himself. He fought with his own body and its sensory perceptions, which is tougher than fighting with outside enemies. The principle of non-violence found its fullest expression in Mahaveera's teaching.

Buddha also preached non-violence and he did not have any objection to eating meat. Mahaveera strongly advocated non-violence and insisted on vegetarian food only. The principles of non-violence apply to microbes also. The devout Jains cover their mouth to avoid killing micro-beings.

Mahaveera and Jainism found a good following among the people. The merchant class was largely attracted towards it. Mahaveera insisted on physical hardship to conquer oneself. He travelled all over India. He might have met Buddha also. There were no contradictions in ther teachings and both of them were beyond any kind of petty feelings.

Kshatriyas could not accept non-violence (both Buddha and Mahaveera were Kshatriyas). Brahmins were dependent on rituals. It was their means of living so the middle class and the merchants found Jainism to their liking. The lower class was not at all bothered. Even today most of the merchants are practicing Jains.

Compared to Buddhism, Jainism had many rules. Buddha was more popular. After Mahaveera, Jainism remained limited to its original adherents. Buddhism kept its doors open and even today you can embrace Buddhism.

After Mahaveera, Jainism had two major divisions. One is called Digambara. Dig means direction and ambar means clothing. For Digambaras east, west, north, and south are their clothing. They do not need clothing so the monks of this division move around naked. Digambara also means naked. The second division is called Shwetambara.

Shweta means white and ambara is clothing. The monks of this division wear white clothing. In Maharashtra where there is a sizeable Jain Community, there are divisions like Chaturtha and Panchama, which literally means fourth and fifth. One of them is a farmer community and the other is a mercantile community. Mahaveera was according to some the founder of Jainism, but the Jain scholars are of the opinion that Jainism is very old.

It began with the first Tirthankara "Adinath" which is also a name of lord Shiva. The word Tirthankara literally means "one who has crossed the holy waters" and the implied meaning is one who has conquered the world or the ways of the world.

The Jain scriptures were written later. They are in Prakrit. They even wrote their own versions of the *Ramayana* and the *Mahabharata*. We get a good record of the Maurya and Gupta times through them. According to the Jain version of *Ramayana*, Ravana was a Jain.

According to their version, Krishna was given initiation by one of his cousins who was known as Neminath. *Mahabharata* calls him Aristnemi. He is a minor character there, but Jains regard him as a Tirthankara. They also give credit to Krishna for building a temple of Tirthankara. This is their way of running down other faiths. Jains also have their own time calculation method, according to which in every age, one Baldeva and one Vasudeva take birth. These are great souls who guide mankind. They have termed both Rama and Krishna as great souls. There is no concept of God in Jainism.

Mahaveera's contribution to India is his advocacy of the principle of Ahimsa or non-violence to the extreme. Anger according to him is the largest enemy of mankind. He himself never got angry with anybody.

Mahaveera ended his life by fasting unto death. Jains do not allow killing of any animal, but the killing of oneself is allowed by them. Jainism remained limited because of the physical hardships. The Jain nuns pluck their hair manually which is a painful process.

According to Stanley Wolpert, Gandhiji used the technique of Mahaveera to fight the British Empire and he used the fasting method to fight with his own countrymen.

This is the story of one great man, who kept growing according to his name "Vardhamana", and who was a great warrior who fought with his own self and emerged a winner true to his name "Mahaveera".

ADI SHANKARACHARYA

&

THE REVIVAL OF HINDUISM

BUDDHISM AND JAINISM were revolts against the caste system and ritualism. Buddha was very popular and he got a huge following. Mahaveera's movement was also gathering momentum. This was a setback for the Brahmin class who had kept their sway. They were helpless now. They could not check Buddism or Jainism. Their 'ism' was apparently on the decline.

In these critical times there rose a man, who was very learned, very intelligent, and a class organizer. To the relief of the priestly class, he was a Brahmin and he adhered to the orthodox Hinduism.

This man, hailing from Kaladi in Kerala, was a phenomenon. He lived a very short life but within this short span of life he did tremendous work.

His energy was almost superhuman and he was like a storm which thoroughly disturbed the religious scenario of India. After Buddha and Mahaveera he was the most influential person who literally uprooted Buddhism with his teachings. This man had many things in common with Buddha so people called him "Prachhanna Buddha". Because of him, India again experienced a revolution.

This was Adi Shankaracharya or Shankara as he is called by the scholars.

Shankara was born to Nambudri Brahmin parents in the year 780 A.D. in a village called Kaladi. Nabudris are known for their knowledge of scriptures and their orthodox nature. Shankara's parents were very poor. Islam had made its entry by this time (the second mosque in the world was erected in Kerala and one of the royals had embraced Islam. These two things had happened in the Prophet's lifetime). Kerala had relations with Arabia from pre-Islamic times. Buddhism had spread far and wide. Kerala had Christianity too. One of the apostles, St. Thomas, was sent to India by Christ himself. So there were Christians from the first century.

So it was high time for a messiah to appear to uplift the ancient religion of India. Hinduism or Brahminism as the scholars called it, was awaiting Shankara.

Shankara was indeed a great soul. He was exceptional right from the beginning. He was a child prodigy. He had learnt by heart all the four *Vedas* when he was still a child and he had started arguing with scholars.

Shankara's father passed away when he was still a child so he was raised by his mother. That was why Shankara was very much attached to his mother. She too was very fond of this extraordinary child. After finishing his education he wanted to learn more from some Guru. For that he had to become a monk. His mother was against that. According to the rules one cannot take a vow of renunciation without one's parents permission. So Shankara had to stay with his mother.

According to a legend one day Shankara went to the local pond to bathe. His foot was caught by a crocodile. People made a lot of noise but the crocodile was not letting him go.

His mother was called. She must have been in a shock to see her dear son about to be dragged away by the crocodile. Shankara was not at all disturbed. His face showed no tension. Shankara said to his mother that if she allowed him to become a monk, the crocodile would let him go. The poor mother understood. It was all Shankara's doing but she was helpless. She had to give permission. Shankara promised her that he would never sever his relations with her and he kept his word.

Shankara took initiation and became a full fledged sanyasi or monk.

According to another legend he saw a scholar immolating himself. That was Kumaril Bhatt, one who had taken a vow that he would revive Hinduism

but who had failed. He was also humiliated by the Buddhist monks. He wanted to kill himself for this failure. Shankara gave a promise to the dying scolar that he would complete Kumaril's unfinished mission.

By this time ritualism had entered Buddhism and Buddha's teachings were completely forgotten. Hinduism had absorbed Buddha as one of the ten incarnations of Vishnu. That nearly finished Buddhism. According to a new story fabricated by the Brahmins, Vishnu decided to be born as Buddha deliberately to mislead the Asuras. He would tell people not to study the *Vedas* and forget about the rituals.

Then Shankara began his historical long march which can be compared to Mao's long march in China. It is chronicled as "Shankar Digvijaya". Digvijaya means victory in all four directions which was carried out by the emperors like Chandragupta or Samudragupta. Shankara was a warrior of wit. He argued publicly with the advocates of other faiths, especially the Buddhists and defeated them. Once they were defeated, they had to accept Shankara's philosophy with their disciples. He defeated them all and made them accept his philosophy which is called "Advait Philosophy". These debates were there right from the beginning, but advaita was associated with Shankara.

According to one legend his fiercest argument took place with Mandan Mishra, who was a staunch Buddhist. The arguments went on for several days and Mandan Mishra was defeated. Before he could surrender, his wife challenged Shankara. She said that as the wife is called the better half, he had to argue with her also. She started asking him about man/woman relationships, carnal pleasures, etc. which he could not answer. He asked her for some time to answer her questions.

According to the legend, he entered the body of a dead king and enjoyed the life of a married man for some time and then again returned to his own body to continue the debate. Now he could answer all her questions and she was defeated. Legends apart, he defeated Mandan Mishra and later Mandan Mishra became one of his staunch followers.

Adi Shankaracharya then established four monasteries in key points of India. In Himalayas, he established one mutt near Badrinath. In the east he chose Jagannathpuri. In the west it was Dwaraka, and in the south at Shrnigeri. These four peethas were called Shankara peethas. The head of each monastery was called Shankaracharya. These four mutts are still there, and they have maintained their records tracing their ancestry to Adi Shankaracharya. Kumaril Bhatta's dream came true; ancient Hinduism was triumphant again.

Shankara's philosophy was taken from the *Vedas*. Even Buddha had agreed with it. "*Ekam sat, Vipra Bahuda vadanti*" which means "Truth is one but the scholars call it by different names". Shankara said that God lives in everything, living and non-living beings.

Human beings suffer because of Maya or illusion which covers everything. He said that we are manifestations of that Supreme Reality called Brahman. But we are covered with this Maya. Once we are rid of that Maya we become Brahman. Then there is no duality. 'A' means no and 'Dwaita' means duality. There is no duality. That is Adwaita.

A legend says that once he met a low caste person in Kashi. He told the person to give way (there were elements of Maya which told him to adhere to the age old caste system). The low caste man answered in Shankara's Adwaita language. He said, "Who should give way? The body or the soul?" Shankara's mind was cleared.

Shankara was a prolific writer. He has written commentaries on the major *Upanishads* and other important religious works. They are called Shankar Bhashyas. They are regarded as authorities on any religious work. Shankara's word is final. His works are still popular and are still read.

Shankaracharya did visit his mother as he had promised. One account says that when his mother died he came to do the final rites. He could not get anybody to help him so he himself cut his mother's body into parts and carried them to the cemetery to do the cremation.

Shankaracharya was an extraordinary scholar but he was not a dry scholar. The hymns that he wrote are very poetic. He wrote that famous "*Chidanandroopam, shivoham shivoham*" which means "I am that eternal being who always remains in a blissful state."

This composition is very musical and the ideas expressed are heavenly. He wrote "*Soundaryalahari*" in praise of the mother goddess which literally moves the reader.

In one of his compositions called "*Devyaparadh-kshamapanstotram*", he prays to the mother goddess to forgive him for the wrongs done because he says, "*Kuputro Jayatequachit, kumata na bhavati*" which means "We have heard that there are many bad sons but there is no bad mother. She is all forgiving."

This warrior monk lived a short life but did tremendous work. After completing his work, he took leave of his disciples and went to the Himalayas. He never returned. That was the end of his physical body but spiritually he will remain alive in the minds of the devout. There is a place near Kedarnath which is called Shankaracharya Samadhi Mandir which is said to be where Shankara spent his last days. It was washed away during the latest Kedarnath tragedy.

VIJAYANAGARA:
THE CITY OF VICTORY

AFTER THE FALL of Prithviraj Chauhan India could not resist the invaders. The invaders came only to loot. None had the desire to stay back in India. The famous Somnath Temple of Gujarat was invaded seventeen times. There was immense wealth in these temples. It is said that the Lingam at Somnath temple was floating. It had no support. It defied the laws of gravity. Mohammad Gazani who destroyed the temple found out that it was there without any support because of magnetic power. He took the sandalwood doors and immense wealth to his capital and developed it. Whenever he was short of money, he came to Somnath and looted it. Somnath was a holy place. In the beginning the Brahmins who worshipped Somnath protested but they were mercilessly killed.

In the year 1206 after Ghori's assassination, Kutubuddin Aibak, who was a slave of Ghori, declared himself as the Sultan of Delhi and thus founded the Slave Dynasty which ruled part of India till the Mugals came. The famous Kutub Minar of Delhi was erected during the times of Kutubuddhin and Altamash.

It was built to give a call for prayers. It was built at the cost of a Hindu temple, which lies in ruins today and is very imposing even in its ruinous state.

This dynasty and the successive Turk and Afghan rulers, calling themselves Sultans, ruled Delhi and surrounding areas for around 320 years. Most of these were religious fanatics.

There was a whimsical Sultan called Mahammad Tughlaq whose whimsies caused the downfall of the sultans. He invaded China and lost an entire army. He shifted his capital to Devgiri of the Yadavas which was renamed Daulatabad. He also introduced copper money in place of gold.

A Hindu prince called Harihara was captured and was forcibly converted to Islam. Harihara then was appointed as a governor. Harihara was reconverted to Hinduism by one the Shankaracharyas.

He waited for an opportunity. When the Sultans became weak, he declared independence with the help of another prince who was called Bukka. They founded the city of Vijayanagara (the city of victory) on the banks of the river Tungabhadra. Vidhyaranya Swami, the Shankaracharya of Shringeri, blessed this new city and the new kingdom. Vidhyaranya, who was known as Madhavacharya, and his brother Sayanacharya were reputed scholars.

About the same time another Muslim kingdom also came into being. This was founded by a man who called himself Hasan Gangu Bahamani. Hassan who had been an orphan was reared by a Brahmin whose name was Gangu.

To express gratitude towards his mentor he called himself as Hasan Gangu Bahamani. Later with his merits he rose to be a noble in the courts of the Tughlaqs. When the Tughlaqs lost their grip he founded the Bahamani dynasty which lasted for two centuries.

These two kingdoms which came into existence at about the same time, fought with each other for survival. The Bahamanis had to retreat because Vijayanagara was very strong and the Bahamanis had to struggle for survival. Later, after the death of Mahamud Gawan, who with his wisdom and bravery had kept the Bahamanis strong, the Bahamanis broke into several dynasties like Kutubshahi, Nijamshahi, and Adilshahi. These factions again started fighting with each other.

Vijayanagara was a big city and was spread over several miles. The fortified city had a million soldiers to defend it. The city itself was well planned. There were many temples with gopuras. There was a market place like the modern market complexes. Now this place is used by a group of people known as Lamanis.

Vijayanagara had commercial relations with foreign countries. The kings were called Rayas and most of them were very cultured. All of them were patrons of the arts and culture.

The most famous of these Rayas was Krishnadevaraya. He came to power after Veer Narsinha. His tenure was from 1489 to 1529. He had to fight many battles with the neighbouring kingdoms. He won all the battles. He defeated the Jihadi army of Mahamadshah Bahamani and his advisor Adilshah in the year 1510.

Like many other Hindu kings he forgave his enemies. After completely routing the Bahamani army he again enthroned Mahamadshah and took the title "*Yavan Rajyasthapanacharya*". He annexed most of the neighbouring kingdoms to Vijjayanagara. He himself was a Kannadiga (from Karnataka) who also knew Telugu. His empire included part of Andhra. Goa was part of Vijayanagara earlier but afterwards it became a Portuguese territory. Krishnadevaraya had good relations with them.

He had Portuguese soldiers in his army. He had sent his envoy to Goa (this envoy was responsible for establishing Portuguese rule in Goa). The Portuguese and Arab travelers who visited this city have written down their accounts.

Krishnadevaraya himself was a man of letters. He has written several books: *Mahalasa Charitra, Satyavadhu Parinaya, Sakal Kathasar Sangraham, Dnyan Chintamani, and Jmbavanti Parinaya.* These are some of the books written by him. He has also written in Telugu which includes a critique on Telugu poets.

A poet, dramatist, an administrator, and a seasoned warrior these were some of the facets of this king. There were eight poets in Raya's court. Tenaliraman was his favourite. There are many stories woven around them which could be the source of Akbar Birbal stories.

Krishnadevaraya passed away in 1529 and with his death the golden era of the Vijayanagara kingdom ended. In 1564 the combined forces of Bahamani factions attacked Vijayanagara. Perhaps there was treachery also. Vijayanagara was defeated. Ramaraya was killed. The city was vandalized and looted by the winners. There was a massacre and later the women were either forcibly converted or sold in the slave market.

Ramaraya's descendents were ruling from Anagondi, which literally means anarchy.

But Vijayanagara still stands there in ruins. As the Urdu saying goes *"khandharko dekhkar pata chalata hai ki imarat kitni buland thi"* which means "One look at the ruins and you are convinced that there once stood a very grand city."

KALIDASA:
THE SHAKESPEARE OF INDIA

WHEN THE GERMAN poet Goethe read the translation of "*Abhidnyan Shakuntalam*" he literally danced with joy. He felt that this play of Kalidasa was a masterpierce, comparable to nothing in any work in any language. He revelled in its poetic expressions. After reading the German translation, he now longed to read the Sanskrit original. He felt that translations leave something out.

Professor William Jones called Kalidasa 'the Shakespeare of India'. He felt that Kalidasa's characterization, poetic expressions were superior to Shakespeare. He also praised Kalidasa's observations about his times.

We call him as Kavikulguru. He was the grandmaster of the poets. He was the Guru whom everybody followed. He excelled in poetry and dramatics. Only seven of his works have survived the ages. They are: *Abhidnyan Shankutalam, Meghduta, Raghuvansham, Kumarsambhava, Ritusanhar, Malvikagnimitram and Vikramorvashiyam.* Kshemendra mentions *Kuntaleshwaradautya* as another work, but this work has not survived.

Unfortunately very little has been recorded about this bard in the annals of history. Something has been gathered from the legends which are popular themes of folklore. Legends cannot be completely believed but we get some elements of truth from them.

According to these legends Kalidasa was an uneducated village youth. Although a very simple and good fellow, he was very dull and was the subject of ridicule among the villagers. There was a princess who was very learned and intelligent. She had decided to marry somebody who was better than her in knowledge, understanding and wit. Many had tried to win her hand in vain. She had humiliated all of them. To teach her a lesson Kalidasa was presented to her as a very learned and witty fellow. By some accident she got married to Kalidasa.

When she came to know about Kalidasa she ridiculed him. It was a big shock to her that she was married to an uneducated, dull commoner.

The crestfallen youth went to a Kali temple and prayed for the whole night to the Goddess. When the Goddess did not respond, he was on the verge of committing suicide. At this time, the Goddess, pleased with the devotion and innocence of the youth appeared before him and blessed him. She endowed on him knowledge, wit, and poetry.

After that he took the name Kalidasa which means "Servant of Kali".

The next morning Kalidasa was a different man. The princess asked him, *"Asti kaschit vagvishesha?"* She was asking him, "Is there anything worth talking about?"

Kalidasa answered in poetry. According to the legends every great work of his begins with the words from this question. The princess was stunned and was very happy. The conversation that followed is recorded in the poetry of Kalidasa.

Kalidasa went on composing great works afterwards. His "*Raghuvasham*" gives the account of the deeds of the kings born in the clan of Raghu, who was the great grandfather of Rama. In later parts it gives the account of Rama's life adhering to Valmiki, but in Kalidasa style. Even the stories of Rama's descendents are given. This has helped the scholars to trace Rama's descendents. It is said that the description of Raghu's battles might be a recollection of Samudragupta's victory over north and south India.

Kalidasa worked as a royal envoy. He was sent on diplomatic missions to distant places. According to some scholars it might be Vidarbha where the kings' daughter was given in marriage. Some think that it might be Ramtek.

Both these places are in Maharashtra, India where he composed *Meghduta*. This composition is about one Yaksha; a celestial being who is away from his beloved who lives in Ujjain. He drafts a letter and dictates it to a cloud.

He tells the cloud how to go to Ujjain and how to deliver the letter to his wife. In one hundred and fifteen verses Kalidasa gives a very accurate description of the route as if he had an aerial view. This description of Ujjain is still applicable to the old part of modern day Ujjain which is called Avantika. This is Kalidasa himself who had been away from his wife.

Ritusanhara gives the description of the seasons of India, called ritus, in one hundred and fifty eight verses.

Vikramorvashim gives the story of Pururava and Urvashi. Here Pururava is Vikrama, who is a mortal, and Urvashi is a celestial dancer who is immortal. Kalidasa took this story from the epics.

Kumarsambhava is the story of Kumar Kartikeya's birth. There are seventeen cantos in this long poem, of which only the first eight are regarded as original. This might be an allegory referring to the famous Gupta king Kumargupta.

Malvikagimitra is based on a real happening. It is a historical account of the love story of the famous Shunga king Agnimitra and Malvika the princess of Malwa. Agnimitra ruled from Vidisha. This proves that Kalidasa's times were after the Shungas.

Abhidnyan Shankutalam is based on the famous story of Shakuntala who was the daughter of Vishwamitra and Menaka. She was reared by the sage Kanva. One day while the sage was away, Dushyanta, the famous king of the Bharata clan came to that place and fell in love with Shakuntala.

They were married and the king went back. Shankutala became pregnant and her father decided to send her to her husband. The husband, Dushyanta refused to accept her. Then she went back and gave birth to a son whom she named Bharata. Later the king again met them and recognized them. This Bharata became a sovereign and India got his name. This story is given in plain words in the *Mahabharata*. Kalidasa has presented it in a very poetic way.

Kalidasa must have travelled all over India as his writings suggest. He seems to be familiar with almost all parts of India. Like Shakespeare, he borrowed all his themes either from *Ramayana*, *Mahabharata* or *Shatpath Brahmana* and 'Kalidasied' them. He seems to be familiar with Bharata's *Natyashastra* because he uses all the figures of speech, all the rasas and he is so famous with simile and metaphor that we have a saying in Sanskrit which says *"upama Kalidasasyas"* - which means there is none like him as far as simile and metaphor are concerned.

The wit of Kalidasa is a subject of legends. He could be given a line and he completed the verse. This is known as samasyapurti (Solution of Problems). Many such samasyapurtis are given in *Bhojprabandha*. Kalidasa could answer any problem.

Historians are not sure about the times of Kalidasa. They have placed him between the first and fourth century. Dr. Raja thinks that Kalidasa lived in the second century. Vaidya feels that Kalidasa lived in the first century.

Dr. Bhandarkar puts him down to the fourth century. Professor Max Muller puts him in the sixth century.

These doubts have arisen because of Kalidasa's works. Kalidasa's *Kumarsambhava* made people think that he might have been in Kumargupta's court. The description of Raghu's conquests given in Raghuvamsha match with Samudragupta's digvijaya mentioned in his inscriptions. So he might have taken inspiration from Samudragupta. Vikramorvashiya mentions Vikrama, Chandragupta II and pays tribute to him in these words, "whose valour or vikrama equaled that of the sun or Aditya." The same words are inscribed on Vikramaditya's coins. Malvikagnimitra is based on the Shunga king Agnimitra so Kalidasa might have been his contemporary.

Kalidasa lived in Ujjain which was the capital of Vikramaditya. His birthplace is shrouded in mystery. They show a place in Ujjain on the banks of river Kshipra which the locals call Shipra.

There is a cave called Kalidasguha. So the locals feel that Kalidasa got blessed in that cave. In Bengal too there are many places associated with Kalidasa. Kali worship has been, and is associated with Bengal. So Kalidasa stories are there in Bengal too. To top this, Kashmir also claims Kalidasa because there too Kali worship was dominant. An inscription in Mandsore also mentions Kalidasa. Vidisha, mentioned in Malvikagnimitra, might be Kalidasa's place.

Whatever place he might have belonged too, the whole of India is proud of this great bard. The whole of India likes to put a claim on him. There was none like him in the past and there will not be any one like him in future.

He was *Ekmevadwitiyam*.

THE RISE AND FALL
OF THE RAJPUTS

THERE ARE MANY stories regarding Rajputs. According to some they were foreign invaders, most probably the Huns, who got settled in Rajastan. These were Hinduised later and were given the status of Kshatriyas. According to another story their ancestor warrior rose from the Agnikunda which might be a symbolic expression for some real story. From this warrior the four major clans of Rajputs emerged. The provice where they settled is called Rajputana. The people who were called Rajputs were headstrong warriors and had many chivalrous qualities in them.

In the sixth century one Brahmin called Guhadatta came to Mevad (then called Medpata) to try his luck. He was a Brahmin by birth and Kshatriya by deeds. He saw that Mevad was a strategic point with the Aravali range on one side. There was no leader for the people. He became their king.

His descendents were called Guhalota which is a Mevadi version of Guhalputra. One of his descendents was Bappa Rawal, who defeated the Mauryas and established his kingdom in Mevad. He is immortalized in folktales. His capital was Chitakuta which became Chitorgad afterwards.

The Anantpura inscription of 912 A.D. gives twelve generations of this Guhalota dynasty. Bappa is not mentioned there but he might be the Khamanna mentioned in it (Bappa is a sort of title).

The Guhalota dynasty had many branches. One was called Meharwal and one was Maharana. Maharana had a Sisodiya branch. Chhatrapati Shivaji claimed descent from this Sisodiya branch.

The Guhalota dynasty changed the capital of Mevad a number of times. But their place of pride was Chitor. Allauddin Khilji attacked Chitor once because he was infatuated with Padmini, the queen of Chitor. He came as a friend of Ratansingh, the king. The popular story says that he wanted to see that exceptional beauty which was not possible. Rajput women wore veils and did not show their faces to strangers. Rajputs never allowed that, but he could be shown the mirror image. According to many the following story is fabricated. Rajputs never allowed such things. They preferred death.

Allauddin was mad with desire. He declared war. Ratansingh fought with him but he was no match for the huge army of Allauddin. He was killed in the ensuing battle.

After Ratansingh, Amarsingh continued but he too was killed. When the fall of Chitor was eminent,

Padmini and other women immolated themselves. This was called Johar. Rajputs were like that. Once they decided to fight, they wore saffron clothes which were called Kesariya and they died fighting. After that the women had to protect their honour by immolating themselves.

Padmini's story might be fabricated but Allaudin's attacking Chitor and winning it is a historical truth. It is also true that the Guhalots gave a tough fight. They never gave up. One of the princes who escaped was Hamir. He continued the war and after some time won back Chitor.

Mevad had many legendary kings. There was Rana Kumbha who had many extraordinary qualities in him. He was a good administrator and a good mediator. He tried to bring all Rajput kingdoms together. He was an architect and he had an ear for music. He was also an acclaimed critic and a playwright too. He was a seasoned warrior who in those times equaled an army. He wrote a commentary on Jaydeva's *Geet Govind* which was much appreciated and was referred to by future scholars. Kumbha's memory is alive in Chitor in the form of Kirtisthambha which is a major tourist attraction. Kumbha met a tragic end. In his old age he became demented and this multifaceted man almost became a lunatic. Finally his own son killed him. It was not for the throne. It was a mercy killing.

After Rana Kumbha, the notable king among the Rajputs was Rana Sangramsinha. He was fondly called

Rana Sanga. Sangram means battle and Sinha means lion. He lived a life true to his name. He ascended the throne in 1509 A.D. He was ambitious and he wanted to expand the Rajput Empire to the entirety of North India. Delhi had become weak. The last of the Sultans and Lodis were fighting with each other, but inspite of that Rana Sanga was not able to win Delhi.

Then Babar, the founder of the Mugal Empire in Delhi, set his eyes on the wealth of Delhi. Sanga thought that with the help of Babar he might be able to rule Delhi. Sanga was to attack Delhi from the southern and western sides. Babar was to storm in from the north. Sanga could not keep his word but Babar attacked according to the plan. His new war techniques and disciplined army defeated the Lodis and Babar became the new ruler. Babar has written in his autobiography that he wanted to rule Delhi. He did not like the people but he liked the land and the nature.

Rana Sanga was disillusioned. He did not expect Babar to stay. In 1557 he challenged Babar. Their armies met at Panipat. The Rajputs fought bravely but they did not get any support from the locals. Babar was determined and his army was disciplined. The Rajputs lost.

This was the beginning of the downfall of the Rajputs. Then in 1567, Akbar attacked Chitor. He knew that Chitor was strategically important.

Once Chitor was subdued, all others would follow suit. But the Rajputs fought very bravely. The battle gave such a headache to Akbar that he ordered the massacre of the thirty thousand defendents of Chitor. Perhaps this was the only event of his life where he was very cruel. Otherwise he was known as a lenient King.

Udaysinha, the Rana of Mevad, had fled before the fort fell. He had taken shelter in the Aravali Hills. There he founded the city of Udaypur.

Udaysinha's son was Rana Pratap Sinha who became immortal because of his fighting spirit and determination. We know him as Rana Pratap. He became King in the year 1572. According to sources he was the eldest son of Udaysinha (Udaysinha had twenty five sons). A popular ballad says,

"Chandra tarai, Suraj tarai, Ulte Ganga dhar
Par Rana Pratapki Zukai nahi talwar
Rajya Jaye to jay Par aan na jane pay
Deshdrohiyonko prabhu Dijo sikh Batay."

Which means:

"The moon may give up her orbit, even the sun may move from his course. The river Ganga may flow in the opposite direction but Rana Pratap's sword will never surrender. If the kingdom is lost, it does not matter but the honour has to be saved. O Lord Rana Pratap give this advice to the people who are betrayers of the nation."

Rana Pratap was determined to take back Chitor. He took a vow that he would keep away from all the luxuries of royal life till he retrieved Chitor. He had all the qualities of Kumbha and Sanga in him but he was more determined.

He took his food in plates made of leaves instead of gold plates. He never slept on luxurious beds. He slept on the floor. His bed was made of grass. Rana Pratap became a legend in his lifetime. There are ballads composed on him which are still sung in Rajputana. Pratap never gave up his fighting spirit. If he had wished he could have become friendly with Akbar because Akbar had given this offer to all and many others had accepted it and were living a peaceful life. But accepting friendship also meant accepting the sovereignty of Akbar which was not acceptable to Pratap.

According to legends, Pratap was a huge man with tremendous physical power. In battles he used every weapon with extraordinary skills. His skill in handling spears was sung by the bards. He used heavy swords (his weapons are still preserved and we wonder how one could lift these weapons and fight with them). His aim never missed and he could cut a horse with a single blow. He had a horse with him which was called Chetak. This horse was very good. It could run very fast and knew the skills to save his master when the time came (there are ballads on this horse also). The horse served its master till death.

Akbar sent Mansing to negotiate with Pratap. Mansingh had given given his sister in marriage to Akbar so he was Akbar's brother in law. He was also very influential as Akbar took his advice on important political matters. Pratap welcomed him and was very polite with him as Mansingh was an elder, but Pratap refused to dine with him because he felt that Mansing had done wrong. He had given up independence and had become a feudal king, and most importantly he had compromised the honour of the Rajputs by giving his sister in marriage. Pratap never forgave anybody who helped the Mugals. Unfortunately Pratap could not bring the Rajputs together. His was a lone fight against a mighty empire.

He gathered the Bhils and the loyal Rajputs and prepared an army. He attacked and disappeared in the Aravalli Hills. This was a guerrilla technique. It is said that once he confronted Akbar and Akbar was well within shot. He could have killed Akbar but the nature of the Rajputs forbade him. He saw that Akbar was helpless so he spared him. In 1576 the Mugal army under the leadership of Salim (who later became Jahangir) met Pratap's army at Haldighat. Pratap was defeated but he could escape. He continued his fight till the end.

Pratap and his horse Chetak have been immortalized in ballads. He became an icon and his story went on to inspire future generations.

The Maharana died without fulfilling his dream, but he died as an independent king.

Mevad was subdued by Shah Jahan when Amarsinha was the king. But the Maharanas never accepted the sovereignity of Delhi. No Maharana visited Delhi. All the descendents of Maharana Pratap followed his ways. Even after the fall of the Mugals, when the British were ruling, they never visited Delhi. It was only after independence that the then Maharana visited Delhi at the insistence and invitation of Pandit Nehru. Panditji himself hoisted the triclour on April 6, 1955.

Maharana Pratap's soul must have felt some kind of consolation in that.

AKBAR THE GREAT

THERE ARE DIFFERENT opinions about Akbar. For some he was great and for some he was just a pretender. Some stories about him are fabricated and some are supported by historical evidence.

His full name was Jalalludin Mohammad Akbar. He was born when his father Humayun was on the run. Humayun was defeated by Shershaha Suri and was refused asylum even by friends. His wife gave birth to Akbar while the defeated and forelorn Humayun had given up all hopes. Humayun regarded Akbar as God's gift. That was why he was named as Akbar. This word is a part of Muslim Prayer "Alla ho Akbar" which means "God is great". This is also a war cry of the Muslims.

Akbar was born in the year 1542 to Humayun and his wife Hamidabanu. Shortly after Akbar's birth Humayun's fortunes changed. The death of Shershah was a godsend. He got his kingdom back but he could not enjoy his kingdom. He died soon.

Akbar showed extraordinary talents right from the beginning. He had teachers appointed to teach him but Akbar had so many doubts in his mind that it was very difficult to satisfy him. The teachers were literally harassed by him, so one by one everybody left. This great Mughal remained illiterate throughout his life.

Akbar had many things in him which made him unique. There was none like him. From his infancy he had to fight for survival. He came to the throne in 1556, when he was just fourteen. There were regents. Bairam Khan looked after him. The affairs of the state were run by this Bairam Khan. He was loyal to the throne but he was very cruel. The people were not happy. Akbar himself found it very difficult to remain under the supervision of Bairam Khan for twenty four hours.

The first revolt came in 1560, four years after Akbar's coming to power. This was by Hemu - a low born servant in the palace who was converted to Islam. He got reconverted to Hinduism. He assumed a grand name like Vikramaditya and declared himself as the new king.

The Mughal army defeated Hemu. He was riding an elephant which is a very inconvenient animal in wars. Hemu was caught and was later beheaded.

This incident gave Akbar an opportunity to remove Bairam Khan. He talked sweetly to Bairam and persuaded him to take a pilgrimage to Meccah. This Guru of Akbar was murdered when he was travelling to Meccah. It is alleged that Akbar was the brain behind the killing.

Akbar's wet nurse Mahim Anga was powerful for a certain period. Akbar regarded her as his mother, and she was influential for a few years. Akbar had to deal with Azam Khan, who was the son of Mahim Anga and who was also dreaming of ascending the throne with the help of his coterie.

Akbar got him killed mercilessly and later built a memorial for him. That ended the *de facto* rule of Mahim Anga.

Akbar planned the expansion of the Mughal Empire in a systematic way. He had many expeditions and he came back victorious. It was not *veni vidi vici* for him. The small kingdoms resisted. He had Gujarat, Kashmir annexed. He defeated all Rajput kingdoms except Chitor.

In 1568, Akbar personally led an attack on Chitor. After the fall of Chitor, he ordered the massacre of its 30000+ defendents. This was the only incident in his life when he dealt cruelly with an enemy.

Like the British governors he waited for an opportunity to annex the kingdoms. His step brother ruled Kabul. After his death Akbar annexed Kabul to the Mughal Empire.

Akbar also came to the south. He wanted Ahmadnagar. Ahmadnagar gave him a tough fight under the leadership of Chandbibi. But Chandbibi was betrayed and he was killed in the battle.

Why are we including Akbar in this book? Akbar despite his foreign descent, was thoroughly Indian. He never regarded India as a foreign land. He was called Mahabali which is a Sanskrit word for a powerful man. He was a connoisseur of arts and culture. He liked the company of learned men. He liked to discuss philosophy. He had studied all religions and he had come to the conclusion that there are many short comings in all religions.

He had nine wise men in his court, whom he called *Navaratnas*. They were picked up by him. He had Mian Tansen in his court who was a great classical singer and composer. Tansen had composed different ragas which are still sung by classical singers. He had Abul Faizi, the poet and Abul Fazal, the historian who wrote *Akbarnama* or the *Times of Akbar*. There was one Raja Todarmal who was his revenue minister. He prepared systematic land records and devised a tax system which is still effective.

One of the Navaratnas was Birbal. There are many stories woven around Akbar and Birbal. They tell of Raja Birbal's extraordinary wit (some of these stories were straightaway lifted from the collection of Tenaliraman stories who was in the court of Krishnadevaraya, the Vijaynagara king). The official records of Akbar do talk about one Birbal who was a warrior and who died at the time of Akbar's Kashmir expedition. According to the stories there was one person named Balvir who later became Birbal. The stories say that sometimes Akbar made wrong decisions and was cruel to the people in momentary anger, but then Birbal, with his wit, corrected them.

Some of these Navaratnas were Muslims and some of them Hindus. Akbar never forced anybody. Mian

Tansen became a Muslim on his own.

Akbar called the learned people of all religions and had debates with them. There is a picture which depicts Akbar having a discussion with Christian missionaries.

Finally he founded his own religion. He called it *Dine Ilahi*. There were a few followers for this religion. This religion died with Akbar.

Akbar established friendly relations with Rajputs. He also married Rajput princesses and allowed them to practice their religions. Rajputs had high ranking positions in his court. Only the Chitor people refused to surrender. The earlier Muslim kings had imposed tax on Hindu pilgrims. He abolished this tax and won the love of his Hindu subjects. Later he abolished 'Jizia' which was a tax on Hindus for practicing their religion. He was against enslavement and had laws against it. Before Lord Bentick, he felt that Sati was a cruel system and he made laws against it (in this tradition, the wife is burnt alive after her husband's death forcefully). According to one historical account he personally rescued one woman who was being taken to the funeral pyre.

Akbar was religious by temperament but he was not a fanatic. He had deep faith in a Sufi saint, Salim Chisti. He named his son as Salim after this saint. He believed that Salim was the result of Chisti's blessings. He built his capital at Fatehpur Shikri. Fateh means victory. He also built a big door there which is called "Buland Darwaja". Akbar began what is called the Mugal style of architecture.

But his son gave him extreme headaches in his last years. Salim revolted against his father. Born of a Hindu mother and a Mughal father, Salim became a fanatic in later years when he became the emperor after Akbar and took the name "Jahangir".

Salim was talked into settlement with his father who had become very frail by that time. He died an unhappy man in 1605 and was buried in the mausoleum built by him.

Akbar is regarded as the greatest among the Mughal rulars. He was lenient, and with the exception of a couple of incidents he never indulged in killing. He tried to bring Hindus and Muslims together. His method was called *rotibeti* wherin Hindus ate rotis (wheat bread) with Muslims and offered them their beti (daughters)(No Muslim offered his beti). He also stopped the influence of the Maulavis (Muslim priests) in political affairs (he himself was a big Maulavi).

He celebrated many Hindu festivals like, Diwali and Holi. He observed Naroz the Parsi festival of New Year. He also used to wear sacred thread like the Brahmins.

An interesting account is given by Henrique who was a part of the Jesuit missionary group who had gone to see the emperor.

"We held some discussions with the Mullas in his presence, but it was he (Akbar) who replied to our most searching questions on behalf of the Mullas, thereby relieving them of much bother and embarrassment, he being gifted with every good sense and understanding, but he did this with excuses and explanations he could best find, so as not to convince (or contradict?) them fully. He is very simple and is very courteous towards everyone, always cheerful, but with a dignity such as one expects from a very great king. He is much loved as well as feared by his people and he is very hard working. To the end he is never idle. He knows a little of every trade and sometimes loves to practice them before his people either as a carpenter or a blacksmith."

KAHAT KABIR SUNO
BHAI SADHO

ACCORDING TO ONE account, in the year 1398, a boy was born to a Brahmin widow. She was not in a position to keep the child, so she abandoned it in Kashi. One Muslim weaver named Neeru found the baby. He had no children. He took pity on the child and brought it home. He reared the child. The child was named Kabir. This is one account of Kabir's birth. According to another account, Kabir was the child of a Nathpanthi couple. But all accounts agree that he was reared by a Muslim couple. They were poor, but very loving and caring.

Being a child of very poor parents, education was not available to Kabir. He did not have formal education. He was illiterate. He himself has written that he did not know reading and writing, and he proudly says that he never came in contact with paper and ink. He learnt from the world. His poverty taught him. The efforts that he had to take taught him. Experience taught him. Even though he was an illiterate person, he was regarded as a very learned man. He had studied every religion and had come to the conclusion that all religions lead to the same eternal reality.

According to one account, Kabir wanted to be a disciple of Ramananda, who was reputed to be a Guru. He was an Advait Vedantee. The problem was he did not accept non-Hindus. One day Kabir lay on the steps of the ghat Ramananda was sure to pass. Ramananda had his bath in the river and when he was returning he stumbled upon Kabir. Kabir clasped his feet and requested him to accept him as his disciple. Ramananda was touched by the humility of Kabir. He accepted him. Kabir's name is mentioned in the list of twelve leading disciples of Ramananda. It might be a fabricated story also because Kabir rose above all his contemporaries and became a legend. And on top of that he was a non-Hindu.

Whatever the truth may be, it is agreed by all that Kabir grew higher than his Guru. He became the advocate of universal religion. His simple language and examples from everyday life, became very popular and he was a bridge between the two communities.

Kabir was for Yoga and Bhakti. He felt one can attain liberation even when one is deeply engaged in his day-to-day affairs. He himself was a married man with a family. He worked on his looms for a living. He had to face the problems one faces when one is living in this world like poverty, misery, etc. Kabir remained content with his life. He had no complaints.

Kabir hated hypocrisy. He was very harsh on those middlemen between god and people. He had Sufi influence on him. He popularized a couplet called Doha, which means two lines. He was very economical with his words. Within a few words he could win the hearts of people. His Dohas are in *"Kabir Granthavali"* and *"Kabir Bijak"* (which also means two lines). He wrote in Purabhi Hindi, which is a dialect of Hindi. He was such a master that Dwivedi calls him "a dictator of the language".

Kabir was a social reformer. He revolted against the monopoly of the so called middlemen. He stressed Bhakti or devotion. He did not like the rigidity that the religions suffered from. He wrote strongly against the false beliefs. He was against fasting and unnecessarily causing hardship to the body. Although he lived in a Tirtha, he felt that there was no need to go on a pilgrimage.

Kabir had a good following. But he never called himself a big Guru, acharya, or Imam etc. One sect which came into being was called Kabirpantha. Dr. Ambedkar's father was a Kabirpanthi and Dr. Ambedkar himself regarded Kabir as one of his three Gurus.

Kabir lived a full life of one hundred and twenty years. He died in 1518. He had both Hindu and Muslim followers. After his death, they fought over whether to bury him or confine him to fire. He was a Hindu and he was a Muslim. But when they lifted the shroud they found flowers inside instead of the dead body.

Kabir would have laughed at them because he had written,

"Jo khoday Masjid basatu hai
Aur muluk kahi kera
Tirath murath Ram Nivasi
Bahar hare ki hera
Purab disha Harika vasa
Paschim allah mukama
Dilare khoj dihime khojou
Ihai Karima Rama
Jeta aurat marad upani
So sab roop tumhara
Kabir pongada Allah ramka
So guru Pir hamara."

Once he said that it was good that he didn't know reading or writing, otherwise life would have been difficult for him. "Dhai akkar Pyarke" is a famous line which says that you do not become learned even after reading a lot of scholarly books. Prem in Sanskrit has two and half syllables which are enough to make you learned.

This great poet influenced many generations. Although he lived in Kashi, all of India knew him. Even today people recite him and quote him. Nobody has spoken as simply and in such a beautiful poetic language other than Kabir. Kabir's dohas are also included in the holy "Guru Granth Saheb". This illiterate man tried to bring Hindus and Muslims together. Just one Doha of his is enough to enlighten the people, as all of them can be said to be storehouses of knowledge.

He considered Kashi and Kaba as the same. Allah was his Guru and Ram was his Pir. This great teacher practiced what he preached. It is said that he went to a place called Megahar to die. People believed that whoever died in Megahar went to hell. They also believed that whoever died in Kashi attained salvation. To prove them wrong he went to Megahar to die. Even in death he was a teacher. Kabir had a son named Kamal who was also a great soul.

It is said that Lord Rama himself, with his brother Laxmana, protected Kabir.

GURU GOBIND SINGHJI

THE BEGINNING WAS from Guru Nanakdev. He was born to Punjabi Khatri (Kshatriya) parents on April 15, 1469. His parents were very poor. They named their child as Nanakdev. This event took place in Nanakana Sahib (this name came later), Rai Bhoi ki Talaundi which is in the Pakistan part of Punjab.

Nanakdev had an insatiable thirst for knowledge. He studied all the four *Vedas* and he also read the holy *Quran*. He became well versed in Hindi, Arabic, and Persian in his childhood. He was seeking answers to the age-old questions. He started asking questions to the people who were regarded as authority. He met sadhus, fakirs, Acharyas and bombarded them with questions.

He had no worldly desires. His father wanted him to settle down in life. He thought that once Nanakdev was married, he would forget all those questions that bothered him. They found a suitable bride for him and had him married. After his marriage Nanakdev had additional responsibilities. He got a job as a "Patwari".

They are revenue department people. He did his job well. Everybody was happy with his work. But Nanakdev remained disturbed. He wanted the answers to his questions.

He used to meditate a lot. And one day he disappeared. Nobody knew his whereabouts. His family was worried. He had gone to a cave where he remained for a whole month. He had decided to find the answers. When he came out he was an enlightened man. He had become Guru Nanak.

It is said that he came out shouting, "No one is Hindu, and no one is Musalman". That was the truth he had found out. The so called religions are only skin deep. The essence is humanity which encompasses all human beings.

The realization came in Sultanpur where he was working as an accountant. Nanak composed hymns, and Mardana - a Muslim family servant composed music. Nanak started a canteen where Hindus and Muslims dined together.

After that Nanak undertook four voyages in four directions. He went east as far as Assam, to the south as far as Ceylon, and to the north up to Tibet. He went to the west also. He visited Meccah, Medina, and Baghdad.

He spent his last days in Kartarpur. He erected the first Sikh shrine there. He nominated Guru Angad as his successor.

This was the beginning of Sikhism.

The scholars are of the opinion that Sikhism was a historical development of the Hindu Vaishnav Bhakti movement. Sikh is a Punjabi word for "Shishya" in Sanskrit, and Sikkha in Pali which means disciple. They are the followers of the Guru. Guru Nanakdev was the first Guru followed by nine Gurus. Guru Nanak believed in the basic principles. He preached what he practiced. He gave five basic principles to his disciples. They are "*Namsankirtana, charity, bath, service and samiran*". Every Sikh has to follow these five principles. He did not believe in rituals. Once he had gone to Kashi where he saw that the Brahmins were offering holy Ganga water. He asked them who they were offering it to. He was told that they were offering it to their ancestors. Then he too started offering holy water. They asked him the same question. He said that he was offering water to his crops in Punjab. They started laughing and asked him, "How can you offer water to your crops in Punjab from here?" Guru Nanak Dev said, "If water offered here can reach your ancestors in heaven, why can't it reach my crops on this planet ?" They got the message.

There were ten Gurus of the Sikhs. The line ended with Guru Gobind Singhji. Two of the Gurus were executed by the Mughals. This initial Bhakti movement became aggressively militant after that.

Guru Gobind Singh started the Khalsa movement in 1699 and called himself as Guru Gobind Singh. Singh means lion. All Sikh men add this Singh to their names. All Sikh women add Kaur to their names which means lioness. Guru Gobind Singh gave a tough fight to the Mughals. Mir, the famous poet, has written about it in his autobiography titled *"Jikre Mir"*. He was surprised to see the emergence of these new warriors who according to him were very peace loving people. Guru Gobind Singh became immortal because of his warrior spirit and organizational skills. He lost his four sons in the battles. He too lost his life. There was an assassination attack on him.

Before his death Guru Gobind Singh gave some rules to the Sikh community. He told them to be disciplined and to continue the fight against fanaticism. He told all Sikhs to keep Five K's with them. They are: Kesa (long hair), Kangi (Comb), Kaccha, Kirpan (a dagger), and finally kird (a bracelet).

Those who are not observing these five Ks are called as patit or fallen ones. The compilation of the hymns composed by the Gurus was done by Guru Angad.

There are 974 verses by Guru Nanak Dev, 64 by Amar Das, 679 by A Das, 2218 by Arjunder, and 115 by Guru Tegbahadur in Guru Granthsahiba. Besides the Gurus there are also verses by Kabir and Namdeo, a Marathi saint poet who had been to Punjab.

Guru Gobind Singh declared that it was the end of the line of Gurus. Thereafter, all Sikhs regard Granthsahib as their Guru. The God himself is a Guru.

Sikhism is monotheistic. They believe in one god. Their favourite words are Satnam karta and Vaheguru. The Sikhs greet each other with *"Sat Shri Akal"* and they remind each other "*Raj Karega Khalsa*" meaning the Khalsa or the pure will reign.

BASAVANNA WHO ALWAYS THOUGHT AHEAD OF HIS TIMES

BASAVANNA OR BASAVESHWARA was the founder of the Veeshaiva or Ligayat Cult. He is fondly referred to as Anna which is an expression used for elder brothers or fathers. Basaveshwara was close to his disciples as he talked to them in their language. Although he was well versed in Sanskrit he chose Kannada to communicate with the people so he could open their hearts and win them. Most of his followers are in Karnataka, Maharashtra, and Andhra. Their origin might have been in Karnataka because most of the Lingayats speak Kannada.

Basavanna has written a lot about himself. His compositions are still read with devotion by the people. There are caste divisions in Lingayats like Teli, Mali, Vani etc. They are, at least most of them are, traders by professions. But all the castes are equal. There is no higher or lower caste. Basavanna did not believe in caste. He wanted to remove those caste distinctions from society. In fact he tried his level best to bring out these reforms centuries ago.

Basavanna was a socialist who lived in the 12th century. This remarkable man fought against all odds in his time. He was a true visionary in the truest sense. He could see the things of the future with his sharp vision. The Marxist scholars have done a lot of research on Basavanna and they have found in him a comrade.

Basavanna was born on Akshaya Trutiya, a very auspicious day for all Hindus, in a Shaivite Brahmin family. When he was twelve years old his thread ceremony was arranged by his parents. Brahmins are called "Dwija" or twice born. Their second birth is at the time of their thread ceremony when they start their formal education. Little Basavanna refused to go through this ceremony. He did not believe in any kind of rituals. Some say that he underwent the ceremony, wore the thread and then cut it, declaring that he was free from any karma.

Basavanna got married to Gangambike. He had a son. Basavanna did not believe in going away from the family and attaining salvation. He was a family man. He was a strong devotee of Lord Shiva, who is also a family man. Lord Shiva is always shown with his wife and two sons. The first son might be absent sometime but the second son Lord Ganesha is always present.

Basavanna believed in pure devotion. He told the people to recite *Om Namh shivay*. Because of his unfailing devotion he was given the name Bhakti Bhandari, which means storehouse of devotion.

He did not write any commentary on any scripture. He advocated something that was unimaginable in those days, and people were surprised. He allowed women to take part in spiritual discussions. He opposed child marriages. He supported remarriages of widows in the twelfth century. This was like dropping a bombshell on society. He openly opposed the caste system. He has written down his discontent in his verse.

"How can one be superior and one inferior when all are the manifestations of the same God?"

His discourses were open to all. There was no caste discrimination in Basavanna's meetings. On top of it, he himself took initiative and arranged the marriage of a Brahmin girl with a low caste disciple of his.

He strongly opposed animal sacrifices. He went ahead and opposed the Yadnya system itself. He said there was no need for any ritual or Karmakanda to attain salvation. Basavanna was a fearless man. There was a warrior spirit in him. He said that doing one's duties and having a total dedication were enough. He laughed at the people who took sanyasa or went to the jungle to do penance. "*Kaykove Kailasa*" was his favourite utterance. It means Kailasa is in your body only. And if Kailasa is there, Shiva is also there within you. Call that Shiva who is within your body and dedicate yourselves to him. That was enough.

In those days he believed that wealth belonged to the society and it should be equally divided among the members of the society. He did not believe that this world is unreal. So he was a materialist and a socialist who was far ahead of his times.

The orthodox people were not happy. They were disturbed and angry. Basavanna had the support of the Bijjala of Kalyan who was a powerful person so they could not do anything and they waited for the correct time. There was a systematic campaign and in time they were able to convince Bijjala that Basavanna was a troublemaker. They also convinced him that Basavanna was a threat to Bijjala.

Bijjala was hesitant because he knew Basavanna's popularity. It was very difficult to do anything to Basavanna. Bijjala sent an army to arrest Basavanna.

Basavanna's followers were ready so when the army attacked, Basavanna's followers literally fought with the army.

Basavanna was very sad because of all this. He told his followers to stop fighting. He left Kalyan and went to Kundala Sangama where finally he took Samadhi. This place is a pilgrimage centre now for all the Lingayats.

Basavanna's followers organized themselves under the banner Lingayata or Veershaiva. Most of them were merchants (Vani), oil makers (Teli), flowersellers (Mali), weavers (Koshti and Sali), etc. Basavanna's philosophy made a deep impact on them. They were happy that they did not have to do anything special.

Basavanna had told them not to observe any riruals. A few rituals are done by a class called Jangam who act as a priest class. But if we strictly follow Basavanna, there is no need of them. Get a linga (Shiva's representation), apply some Bhasma (ash) on your body and go on doing your daily work with a firm faith in Shiva.

Utter the name of Shiva as many times as possible. There is no need to go to an isolated place also. Basavanna united the people and gave them easy ways.

Basavanna erected Shivanubhavamantapas where people could gather and discuss any religious issues. He told his followers to keep away from mourning. So if there is a death in the family, Lingayats do not mourn.

Basavanna's works are in Kannada. They are *Shatsthala Vachana, Kaladnyana,* and *Shikharathrachana.* There was no biography written by his immediate disciples. His biography was written much later by one Shankaravadhya called Basava Purana. There is one in Kannada and one in Telugu.

Basavanna's sect was joined by Allamprabhu and then Akkamahadevi, both of whom continued the work of Basavanna in the social sphere as well as in the literary sphere (Akka Mahadevi is regarded as the incarnation of Mother Goddess).

Basavanna lived a short life (1131-1167 A.D.), but in 36 years he brought in a revolution. India will forever remember this rebel.

Basavanna's Jayanti is celebrated at three places: Ulavi in Karwar, Bagewadi where he was born, and Basavakalyana where he spent most of his life.

Basavanna's followers think that he was an incarnation of Shiva himself. There are stories of miracle, like the river Krishna making way for him or him transforming the contract killers into Lingayatas etc, but if you truly follow Basavanna you don't pay any attention to them.

Basavanna gave importance to Linga Puja. He was not the first one. Linga puja is the oldest form of idol worship in the world. Shiva is always worshipped in Linga form. There are Shaivites, but Basavanna gave a new dimension to Shiva worship. He said that one doing his duty is worshipping Shiva. He need not do anything else.

He gave the message of Gita in different understandable words.

Thank you Basavanna.

SHIVAJI NA HOTA TO
SUNNAT HOTI SABKI

CHHATRAPATI SHIVAJI WAS a phenomenon. You won't find the likes of him elsewhere. There were great kings, great warriors, great administrators, great thinkers, great strategists, and great human beings. But in Chhatrapati Shivaji we find all the qualities. None was so effective, none was so much remembered, and none is so much idolized. I hail from Kolhapur where Shivaji's descendents ruled up to independence. Nearby is Satara, where another branch of Shivaji's family ruled and then there is Pune where there are many legends about Shivaji. Pride is a small word as far as Chhatrapati Shivaji is concerned for the people of Kolhapur. Here everything is named after Shivaji. There is a Shivaji Chowk, Shivaji Putala.

If some places are yet to be named, they will be named either after Shivaji or any of his descendents like Sambhaji, Shahu or Shahaji, etc. There are some people in Maharashtra who have started a religion in Shivaji's name. They were so venomous in language that even Chhatrapati would have been disgusted because he was lenient even towards his arch enemies. Shivsena started by Balasaheb Thackrey was a movement to reckon with and it became a party afterwards. They ruled Maharashtra for some years.

Shivaji was born to Shahaji and Jijabai Bhonsale on Shivneri fort in 1630. There are doubts about his birthdate. People celebrate it on one day and the Govt. celebrates it on another day. Shahaji was a feudal lord who served different masters at different times. Besides Jijabai, he had other wives and also sons from them. Shahaji had strained relations with his father-in-law, Lakhuji Jadhavrao of Sindhkhed Raja. It was during battle time that Jijabai had to take asylum on Shivneri Fort. The goddess of that fort was Shivai so Shivaji was named after her.

As Shahaji was passing through difficult times, he had no time for his son or Jijabai. So Jijabai reared the son. Shivaji was brought up in Pune. One person named Dadoji Konddev looked after the land affairs of Pune.

Earlier they regarded him as a teacher of Shivaji. But afterwards, because of the anti-Brahmin lobby of the scholars, they denied that place to Dadoji. The matters went to such an extent that they removed even the statue of Dadoji.

We can say that his mother Jijabai was a woman of strong character and played a big role in the making of Shivaji.

At the age of sixteen Shivaji decided to build his own kingdom and started with a fort that was nearby.

He got the support of the local Marathas called Mavlas (the whole province was called Maval and the residents were called Mavlas). He had a small army of them. They were loyal, headstrong, and very brave. Systematically he started building his own kingdom.

Shivaji had to fight with the established Muslim kingdoms like Adilshaha of Vijapur (his father served with them). Sometimes Shivaji retreated and sometimes he was aggressive. Sometimes he compromised and when the time came he retrieved whatever was lost. The Adilshaha sent his army and seasoned waariors to fight with Shivaji. In one instance a very strong warrior called Afzal Khan cornered Shivaji. Shivaji played his tactics. He gave the impression that he was about to surrender and was interested in peace talks. A meeting was fixed at Pratapgad. At the time of meeting Afzal Khan tried to kill Shivaji with his bear hug (Afzal Khan was a massive man with big physical strength). Shivaji was prepared. He was wearing a weapon on his hand called "waghnakh" which literally means tiger's claws. He killed Afzal Khan with those claws. Afzal's unaware army was defeated (Khushwant Singh referred to this act in derisive terms and the Marathas were angry with him). There are many instances in Shivaji's life where he displayed extraordinary courage and understanding. He knew that prudence was the better part of valour when time required it.

One time his father was imprisoned by the envious nobles in the court of Adilshaha. Shivaji used the powerful Mughals and had his father rescued.

Once when an army was on his chase he misguided them by sending a flock of bulls with torches tied to their horns. Shivaji was elsewhere but the chasing army thought the torches were held by Shivaji's men. And Shivaji was safe. This is known as the Katraj Ghat incident.

He fought with the mighty Mughals also. He could have been caught by them in Pune, but he and his men disguised themselves as marriage party members and Shivaji attacked the Mughal general who was staying at Lal Mahal, Shivaji's palace. The sleeping general who was Shaistekhan was caught unawares. He escaped through the window but in the flight, Shivaji cut his fingers.

The last powerful Mughal emperor Aurangzeb was very upset by Shivaji's activities. Shivaji had been successful in subduing small Muslim Kingdoms and he had made inroads in Mughal provinces also. He was a force to be reckoned with and Aurangzeb now regarded him as a threat.

A big army was sent from Delhi to defeat and capture Shivaji. Shivaji lay low but the Mughal army was determined. A Rajput king named Mirza Raje Jaysingh negotiated and he promised that if Shivaji surrendered he would get some feudal position in the Mughal court. According to him this was a lucrative offer.

Shivaji was never interested in getting feudal positions. He was determined about his own kingdom which he called "Hindavi Swaraj". Swaraj means self rule.

According to Mahadev Govind Ranade, Shivaji was a phenomenon brought in by the saint poets of Maharashtra who had been trying to awaken the people since the twelfth century. This in no way diminishes the glory of Shivaji. The making of Shivaji was a phenomenon unparalleled.

Anyway, Shivaji was persuaded to appear in the court of Aurangzeb where he was treated like any ordinary noble and later was put under house arrest in Agra. Shivaji was there for a few days along with his son but he escaped. He pretended to be ill and then he started receiving boxes. Everyday the boxes were checked. When they were sure that there was nothing suspicious in the boxes they stopped checking. And one day Shivaji and his son escaped in the boxes. This escapade has been the theme of many ballads and plays.

Shivaji decided to coronate himself as Chhatrapati after this incident. Again some Brahmins objected but Shivaji got the sanction from the Kashi Brahmins.

Shivaji died in 1680 at the age of fifty. He had a fall from his horse and that was the cause of his death.

Shivaji was remarkable in many aspects. Shivaji's emergence was a Hindu outburst but Shivaji was not a fanatic. He rebuilt some of the vandalized temples but he never retaliated.

In fact he was as reverent towards Muslim shrines as he was to Hindu temples. He never destroyed any mosque or Darga. He was respectful towards all religions. Once his army attacked and won Kalyan's treasury carrying unit. Along with the loot they also brought the daughter-in-law of the subhedar or the officer of the fort. Shivaji was very polite towards her and he sent her back in a dignified way.

Shivaji dealt with the British also. He looted their depot in Surat. He was not vengeful.

Shivaji was the first to realize the importance of a naval force. He built his own naval force under Kanhoji Angre. He personally supervised the construction of Sindhudurga, a sea fort which is still strong and where the footprints of Shivaji are still preserved.

He was very reverent towards the saints. Ramdas and Tukaram were his contemporaries. Ramdas has written about him. The anti-Brahmin lobby had been trying to prove that there was no connection between the two. There was definitely a connection because in his last years Shivaji had sent his son to Ramdas. Anyway, Ramdas was a politically conscious saint.

Many centuries have passed but Shivaji remains alive in the minds of people. He might have spent most of his life in Maharashtra but he belonged to the whole of India. It is wrong to term him as a Maratha warrior only.

Shivaji belonged to the whole of India. He is a national icon.

CHHATRAPATI SAMBHAJI
(1657 - 1689)

ANOTHER GLORIOUS PAGE of India's history was written by Chhatrapati Sambhaji who was the eldest son of Chhatrapati Shivaji and his successor. Compared to his father Sambhaji, he lived a short life. He was tortured and killed by Aurangzeb who came down to subdue the Marathas. During his short tenure Sambhaji did a lot. He was a brave warrior and an able administrator but his image was maligned by the Mughal and later British historians.

Shivaji had many wives. Sambhaji was born to Saibai. Sambhaji grew up under the care of his grandmother who had also brought up Shivaji. Sambhaji was the eldest. After some years a son was born to Soyarabai (another of Shivaji's wives). This was Rajaram. Sambhaji was brave and headstrong. He lacked the prudence of his father. He had many other qualities in him. He knew many languages and he could write. He was a tall and well built person who liked to go hunting. There are some legends about his love-life which may or may not be true. But Shivaji was disturbed by his son's aggressive nature. There are some compositions in Sambhaji's name. He liked the company of poets. One poet named Kavi Kalash was his lifelong companion.

Here are some compositions of Sambhaji.

"Sasu kahe dadhibechanko
Sukhad sukhdai kahan te ghou hakro
Mohimile 'Nrup Shambhu' gupal
Tamal tarei vah gail jo sankarou.
Mo tan taki badi akhiyan te
Lei phir mo tan dhakri
Kankari odi gayi par te pai
Kareje kahan dhou gadi kankari."[2]

The translation of the above composition:

"Her mother in law had sent her to sell curds, when Krishna called her. She was very happy and said 'I met my Gopalkrishna in a narrow lane near the tamal tree. He was staring at my body. He tossed a little piece at me and now it is deposited in my heart."

Sambhaji wrote poems when he was busy in his expeditions. His poems are romantic and there are theosophical notes present. This trend continued till his end.

[2] KAMAL GOKHALE, '*Shivputra Sambhaji*', page 426

Because of Sambhaji's daredevil nature, Shivaji was worried. After coming of age, Sambhaji revolted against his father and joined the Mughal prince who had come on an expedition

But Sambhaji realized his mistake and returned home. Shivaji could not trust him fully. On top of that there were a number of people who did not want Sambhaji to succeed Shivaji. They kept on plotting against him. It was believed that his step mother Soyarabai was leading those people who did not like Sambhaji.

At the time of Shivaji's death, Sambhaji was not by his bedside. His opponents had managed to keep him away but as soon as he got the news, Sambhaji rushed to Raigad, Shivaji's capital and ascended the throne.

It is written that Sambhaji did not forgive anybody who plotted against him. Some of the loyal aides of Shivaji were also killed. Amongst them was one Annaji Datto. It was believed that Sambhaji did not even spare his step-mother Soyarabai. He punished her and gave her the death sentence. But now it has come to light that Soyarabai was alive for many years after Sambhaji's coronation. He also massacred Shirkes who were his relatives and who had plotted against him. The word Shirkan means the massacre of the Shirkes, but recent investigation says that Shirkan means the 'land of the Shirkes'. So Sambhaji might not have killed him.

Sambhaji continued his father's strategies. The Maratha Empire was to stay. He continued his expeditions.

He wanted to complete his father's mission. He turned his attention to Goa. He had decided to oust the Portuguese from Goa. He came with his full army. He built a fort in Ponda. The Portuguese were so scared that the then governor rushed to old Goa to pray. He put the royal insignia before St. Xavier's coffin. Sambhaji cancelled his expedition on account of two things: the river was full and because of the speed of the water, the horses could not go foreward. Sambhaji himself would have drowned if his loyal aide had not caught hold of him.

The second reason was that the Mughals had come in full force and were plundering the Maratha territory.

Sambhaji with his brave lot, gave a tough fight to Aurangzeb. Aurangzeb was surprised because he knew that wars cost money and the Marathas were incessantly making wars. The Marathas were tough warriors. They had full faith in their king. They resorted to surprise attacks. The guerrila warfare of the Marathas caused a lot of headaches for Aurangzeb.

Sambhaji was caught by Aurangzeb in Sangamashewar. He was not hiding as some people thought. He was tired and was taking a rest in a temple. According to Vasant Kanetkar, Aurangzeb wanted money. As Sambhajji was fighting with Aurangzeb for many years, Aurangzeb thought he had money. When Sambhaji could not give any answer, he was tortured. He was blinded and his hands were cut off. Finally, after many days of torture, he was beheaded. Kanetkar had done research on Sambhaji when he was working on his plays "*Raigadala Jevha Jag Yete*" and "*Ithe Oshalala Mrityu*" which were based on Sambhaji's life.

According to one account, Sambhaji was asked to embrace Islam. His reply was that he would embrace Islam if he got married to Aurangzeb's daughter.

Whatever might be the truth, there are many grains of truth in the stories around Sambhaji. Both Shivaji and Sambhaji were religious but were not fanatics. Both of them were seasoned warriors. Both of them were good administrators.

The similarities end there. Sambhaji was headstrong when Shivaji was not. Sambhaji lacked the cunning of Shivaji. Shivaji knew when to retreat and when to strike.

Sambhaji had something more. Unlike his father, he was a man of letters. He was a poet and he could compose. Shivaji had no time for these activities. Sambhaji had the time in his adolescent years. He also liked the company of wise men and poets.

Sambhaji is remembered for many things. His Goa expedition would have changed the course of history, had it been successful. His martyrdom has been the subject of poems for centuries. They call him Dharmveera Sambhaji.

So let it be Dharmaveera.

RANRAGINI TARABAI
(1675-1761)

IF YOU GO to Kolhapur via Belgaum, you are welcomed by a huge statue of a woman on a horse. The horse has raised his front legs and the statue is balanced on the hind legs. The woman who is on the horse has raised her sword in an aggressive manner. She is warning her enemies, "If you caste an evil eye on my Kolhapur, this sword will take care of you".

This woman is Tarabai. She was the daughter in-law of Shivaji. She was the wife of the second son of Shivaji, Rajaram.

Sambhaji's arrest and subsequent death was a big blow to the Marathas. Sambhaji's wife Yesubai and son Shahu were also caught. Aurangzeb did not kill them; they were kept in the emperor's house and were personally looked after by Aurangzeb's daughter.

When the Marathas were leaderless, Rajaram was crowned as the new king. He was a sick man and fighting was too much for him. He died because of the strain that was put on him by history. He could neither become like his father, nor could he emulate his brother, Sambhaji. Both his father Shivaji and his brother Sambhaji were extraordinary men. But in this critical time he had to manage their affairs.

It was Tarabai who took over after his death. She was the daughter of Hambirrao Mohite, a valiant Maratha General. Rajaram died in 1700, which was the beginning of Tarabai's career. After her marriage with Rajaram, the turn of the events trained her for future leadership.

As Sambhaji's son and wife were detained by Aurangzeb; Tarabai who had a son felt that her son was the rightful king. She was an excellent negotiator. She talked to the Maratha stalwarts who mattered, coronated her son, and started ruling the Maratha kingdom from Panhala, a fort near Kolhapur. She wanted Aurangzeb to support her claim. When he did not, she declared war against him.

Tarabai was a good administrator and an excellent strategist. She herself went to the war front and gave guidance to the generals. This daughter-in-law of Shivaji had all the military talent of her great father-in-law. She won back all the Maratha forts captured by the Mughals.

To check the Maratha unity, the Mughals released Shahu (Sambhaji's son). When Shahu returned, the Marathas were confused. Shahu appointed Balaji Vishvanath as his prime minister. He was very efficient. He talked with all those Maratha warriors who were earlier on Tarabai's side and took them on Shahu's side. Then it was an open confrontation between Shahu and Tarabai. Shahu was on the winning side. In the meantime, another wife of Rajaram who was equally ambitious arrested Tarabai and her son; Shahu released them. The Maratha Empire was now divided in two. Shahu ruled from Satara and Tarabai ruled from Kolhapur. She tried to bring the two kingdoms together by making Shahu adopt her grandson.

Tarabai fought valiantly and kept the Maratha spirit alive for seven years. She rose above all others in this period. She was a terror to the Mugals and her enemies. When India's history was written, one just couldn't forget those seven years.

Unfortunately after Shahu's coming back, Tarabai had to fight with her family members. If the Marathas had remained united at this critical hour, history would have been different.

Before her death, she got the news of Panipat's third battle in which the Marathas lost. It was a routing victory for the other side. Many Maratha warriors lost their lives. It was a terrible blow for the Marathas. When this brave fighter heard the news, her earlier spirit died, and a new Tarabai, who was nothing like her old self, said, "It is good that they lost!"

BAJIRAO PESHWA THE FIRST
(1700-1740)

BALAJI VISHVANATH BHAT from Shrivardhan left his native place and came to Satara. He did some petty jobs in the beginning. He worked for Tarabai also for some time before joining the Shahu Camp. Once he joined Shahu, he brought many other Maratha stalwarts to the Shahu Camp. Shahu came to know about his abilities and in no time he became the most trusted man of Shahu. In 1713 he was appointed as "Peshwa". Balaji was first stationed at Saswad near Pune. Balaji did many things for Shahu, and only because of him Kanhoji Angre, the naval lord joined the Shahu camp. He was also instrumental in the affairs of Delhi. He acted as a king maker. He brought a lot of ransom money to the Maratha treasury. This founder of Peshwai died in 1720.

Balaji's eldest son was Bajirao the first. His other names were Visaji, Bajirao Ballal and the Elder Bajirao. He used to go with his father on expeditions. Shahu had seen his talent so he appointed him as Peshwa after Balaji Vishvanath's death.

A Nijam was cunningly refusing to pay taxes. Bajirao clashed with him and won the battle; the Nijam surrendered and Shahu's sovereignty was accepted by him.

After that he targeted the whole of north India. His valiant brother Chimajiappa subdued Gujarat. In the meantime, the army chief of Shahu plotted against the Peshwas and Bajirao had to deal with him.

He sent Chimaji to oust the Portuguese from the Maratha provinces and so Chimaji ousted the Portuguese from Thane and Vasai.

Bajirao is remembered for his fighting spirit. Most of his life was spent in fighting with the enemies of the newly founded Maratha Empire.

He used to say that instead of cutting the branches one must cut the roots. He defeated the Mughal Governor of Malwa. He helped Chatrasal (a poet) of Bundelkhanda. Chhatrasal had written,

"Jo gati graha gajendraki;
So gati bhai janu aaj
Baji jat Bundelki,
Rakho Baji laj."

Bajirao was a speedy general. He was always on the move. His war strategies were superb. Finally after facing defeats at many fronts, the Mughals surrendered and there was a treaty between the Mughals and the Marathas. Nijam was a big enemy. He was defeated a number of times by Bajirao but the Nijam had a policy of talking peace and again attacking. At one time they led a massive army of Mughals but Bajirao still defeated him.

Bajirao was a good general and a valiant soldier. He fought alongside his soldiers. He treated all his soldiers with kindness. He trained a new batch of Marathas like, Shinde, Holkar, and Gayakwad who later established their own kingdoms.

Bajirao's military strategies have been praised by British historians also.

When he was in Bundelkhand, he met Mastani, an exceptional beauty. Mastani never left him. Bajirao was a Brahmin and Mastani was a Muslim. It became a big issue in the city of Pune. Bajirao's brother and son tried their level best to separate these two but were unsuccessful. He loved Mastani very much and she accompanied him on all his expeditions. There was a palace built for her in Pune. Mastani became a legend in her lifetime.

Bajirao died at the age of forty. He died of a fever.

Bajirao, the first or Elder Bajirao, established the Maratha Supremacy in India. The Mughals had bigger armies, a lot of ammunition and guns, but Bajirao could defeat them easily. He is compared with many other generals but Bajirao is unique because he never lost a battle. Chhatrasal whom he helped has written:

"Jagme dwei upaje Brahman
Brugu aur Bajirao

Un dhai Rajputiya
In dhai Turkav."

The meaning is, "Ony two Brahmins were born here. One was Parashuram and the second was Bajirao. The first one annihilated the tyrant Kshatriyas. The second one killed the Turks."

Bajirao could have enthroned himself, but he never did. The Mughals and the other mighty forces were helpless before him. Even the Chhatrapati were helpless but Bajirao remained loyal. This quick tempered Peshwa was very loving. He won every battle but he lost on the home front.

Bajirao became an adjective in Marathi Language. If somebody thinks very highly of himself, People say, "Who do you think you are, Bajirao?"

But there is no equal of Bajirao.

THE BHAKTI MOVEMENT

ACCORDING TO MAHADEV Govind Ranade, the Bhakti Movement that rocked the whole of India was a purposeful movement. It was a well laid out plan to awaken India. The powerful churning of the thought process acted as causative factors. The later rise of the Marathas can be linked to that. This movement started somewhere around the eleventh century and is still in continuation. Most of the saint poets excepting Ramdas were not at all bothered about political upheavals. They remained immersed in Bhakti or devotion. They composed and sang songs. They brought the people together. The whole Hindu community got involved in this. The differences were forgotten. The Bhakti movement crossed the boundaries of Hinduism, Jainism, Lingayats and even Muslims. There were Sufi saints who were influenced by the Bhakti movement. Kabir, Mira, Surdas, Tulsidas, Rahim; all went on awakening the people and bringing them together. Sufis were Muslims and they had firm faith in Islam, but they took some of the elements of the Bhakti movement.

Among the first exponents was Gorakhnath. He was the disciple of Macchindranath (who was supposedly a disciple of Lord Shiva himself). Macchindranath is the founder of the Natha Cult which later merged into the Bhakti movement. There is no literature available on this first Nath but a lot of compositions of Gorakhnath are available. Gorakhanath was a good organizer and he toured the whole of India. He composed in many languages. Gorakhpur, which is named after him, is a city on the Indo-Nepal Border. But the influence of this Nath is seen in all parts of India. The Nath cult still survives. They are followers of Yoga, and it is a tough belief. There are Nine Nathas whose biographies are written down by their disciples. Some of them have Muslim influence in them.

The Bhakti Movement is also known as the Bhagavata Cult. According to some scholars this cult grew in the times of the Guptas because most of the Gupta kings called themselves "Param Bhagavata". According to V. R. Shinde, this cult is pre-Vedic. The earlier Sun worshippers later became Bhagavatas. Bhagavan is the title of the Lord. Bhagavatas are Vaishnavites. Vishnu is one of the names of the Sun. Later the Bhagavatas concentrated on Shri Krishna, the eighth incarnation of Lord Vishnu. So for the Bhagavatas the *Bhagavad Gita* is the scripture.

This movement was spread all over the country. In the north, Kabir, Mira, Tulsidas, Surdas, and many others popularized this movement.

In Bengal, Chaitanya Mahaprabhu took this movement to the masses. In Maharashtra and Karnataka a number of saint poets emerged. At the centre was Shri Krishna, in the form of Vittala of Pandharpur. Further south, Tirupati Balaji and Shri Krishna of Udupi were worshipped and a mass movement was born. In Pandharpur, the devotees gathered in the Month of Ashad, roughly around August/September. This is observed every year. Nobody knows when this began. From many villages and towns and cities, the devotees proceed towards Pandharpur in groups. This is called Dindi. People from different castes of Hinduism forget their differences and go singing and dancing to Pandharpur. They mostly walk. The villagers take care of their food and shelter. After arriving at Pandharpur, all Dindis become one, and after visiting the temple they disperse.

These Dindis go on singing the compositions of the saint poets. According to some this must have begun after Dnyaneshwar. But according to Dnyaneshwari Dindi was prevalant even before the times of Dnyaneshwar. The temple and deity are older.

The story of Dnyaneshwar is very interesting. One Vitthalpant Kulkarni, who was married to one Rukmini, left his house and became a sanyasi. When his Guru came to know that Vitthalpant had taken sanyasa without prior permission of his wife, he sent him back. A sanyasi becoming a householder was unheard of.

The orthodox Brahmins declared him to be an outcaste. This sanyasi turned householder had four children. He asked the elders of the community to take him back to society. He was told that his death was the only way. Both Vitthalpant and Rukmini committed suicide and left their children at the mercy of society. The four children, Nivrutti, Dnyaneshwar, Sopan and Muktabai were extraordinary. They went to Paithan (the ancient city of Pratisthan) and had themselves re-entered into the Brahmin community. Nivrutti got initiated by Gahininath, one of the Naths and he initiated his brothers and sisters into the Natha cult.

All four of them have composed in Marathi. But Dnyaneshwara became famous because of his commentary on the *Bhagavad Gita*. He called it *Bhavarth Deepika* but it is commonly known as *Dnyaneshwari*. This was written in Ovi meter and was in colloquil Marathi. The earlier commentators had written their commentaries in Sanskrit. This was the first attempt to bring something sacred into the people's language.

Dnyaneshwara has written some more books. *Changdev Pasashti* and *Amrutanubhava* are two of them. He wrote these two at an early age.

He acknowledged Shankaracharya's commentary on the *Gita* but *Dnyaneshwari* is his own work. His parents' names are symbolic of the deities in Pandharpur. Even the names of the four children represent something. For example, Nivrutti is renunciation, Dnyan is knowledge, Sopan is step, and Mukta is salvation or freedom.

He decided to end his life at the age of twenty one by Samadhi method. In Samadhi, an underground room is prepared and when the person enters, the room is closed from above. His contemporary Namdev has given an eye witness account of his Samadhi.

Nivrutti, Sopan, and Mukta have also written accounts of the Samadhi. All four of them did their level best to popularize the Bhakti movement.

It was a time when every caste had a saint poet and each one tried to bring his or her folks in this movement. Gora Kumbhar was a potter, Sawata Mali was a gardener, Sena Nhavi was a barber, Kanhopatra was a courtesan, and Shaikh Mahammad was a Muslim. Their compositions are in Marathi and they revolve around Vitthala, the presiding diety of Pandharpur.

In one composition, Bahinabai, a disciple of Tukaram wrote, "Dnyandeve rachila paya" which means that Dnyaneshwar laid down the foundations for this Bhakti movement.

But the real founder and organizer was Namdev, Dnyaneshwara's contemporary. Namdev was a tailor by profession and his whole family was immersed in devotion. His father, mother, children and his maid Janabai all of them were devotees of Vitthala and have written abhangas.

It is said that Namdev composed songs and sang them. People attended his Bhakti sessions and even Vitthala attended those sessions.

It was Namdev who went to the north, to popularize the Bhakti movement. He stayed in Punjab for a while and has written something in Punjabi. Namdeva's compositions are included in the *Guru Granth Sahib* , the scripture of the Sikhs. He is the only Maharashtrian to figure in the *Guru Grantha Sahib*.

These Bhakti poets brought the people together. They might not have been successful in the annihilation of the caste system, but at least they succeeded in bringing these different sections together. Twice a year they meet in Pandharpur and the tradition is still prevalant.

After Namdev it was Eknath who led the Bhakti movement. Eknath was a disciple of Janardan Swami. He composed a lot; he wrote on the *Ramayana*. He also composed some Bharuds, which are sung even today by illiterate masses. Eknath had many qualities in him. It was a time of Muslim invasions and Eknath wanted the Hindus and Muslims to be united. He wrote on the good points of both religions.

He criticized those who were orthodox and were foolishly following meaningless rituals. Like all reformers, Eknath was also harassed by the orthodox. He believed that all are children of the Almighty and there should not be any discrimination on account of caste. It is said that Eknath even dined with the untouchables. Once when he was taking Ganga water to Rameshwar, he saw a thirsty donkey. He felt pity for that and he poured the holy water in the mouth of that donkey. Eknath was among the rare saints who practiced what they preached.

Eknath has also written in Hindi. His gavalans and bharuds are still sung by the villagers in Maharashtra.

BHAKTI MOVEMENT II

THE BHAKTI MOVEMENT churned society for more than five centuries and awakened the collective conscience of people and perhaps gave rise to movements that shook India. Vidhyaranya and his brother Sayana were Sanskrit scholars who took the lead in the foundation of the Vijayanagara Empire. Vijayanagara also houses a Vitthala temple (without an idol) which survived vandalism. The most famous king of Vijayanagara, Krishnadevaraya was a poet and he has penned some Bhakti literature. The Maharashtra saints did not get involved in political movements but their words did the magic. Mira the saint poet of Rajputana was connected to both Rana Pratap (who was her kin) and also Akbar who was fond of the compositions of Mira and it is said that he attended some of her Bhakti sessions. Shivaji the Great was very fond of holy men and many a time he risked his life to attend the sessions of these Bhakti poets.

In Karnataka, Purandaradas and Kanakdas, the Virshaiva poets, Shri Vadiraj Swami and Shri Raghavendra Swami, did the awakening. They wrote in Kannada, the local language and touched the hearts of the people.

The credit goes to Shri Vitthala, the presiding deity of Pandharpur. Shri Vitthala acted as a link between Maharshtra, Karnataka, Goa, and Andhra. According to scholars he was worshipped by the aborigines in the beginning. Later he was Hinduised. His original nature is closer to Shiva, but later he became a Vaishnava deity and was regarded as a form of Shri Krishna, the eighth incarnation of Lord Vishnu.

All these saint poets were aware of the problems of the people and they wrote extensively on them.

One shining example is saint Tukaram. He was not a Brahmin. He belonged to the Maratha caste. But his family was in the grocer's business. Tukaram liked to go to a small hill which was near his village Dehu (he attained realization there). Tukaram had many mystical experiences. He was a devotee of Vitthala. His Guru Baba Chaitanya did not meet him physically but gave him the mantra "Jay Jay Ramkrishna Hari" in Tukaram's dream.

Tukaram composed abhangas and sang them. Because of his plain but true words, he became very popular. The orthodox Brahmins could not tolerate his popularity. He was harassed by them and was told to drown his notebooks of abhangas in the Indrayani River. According to legends, nothing happened to the notebooks and they were retrieved intact after a few days. There are two explanations. One is that the story is symbolic. The second explanation is that Tukaram might have written them on oilskin paper.

Anyway the moral of the story is Tukaram's abhangas survived and they are still on the lips of the people.

Tukaram was a rebel with a cause. He did not like rituals and hypocrisy. He wrote extensively on them. He has written:

"Vedancha to arth amhasich thava/Yerani vahava Bhar Matha."

Which means, "We know the true meaning of the *Vedas*. Others are there as load bearers". He was referring to the Brahmins who preserved the *Vedas* through oral traditions for centuries without bothering about the meaning.

Tukaram's words angered the orthodox Brahmins who had a monopoly on learning scriptures. Here was a so called Shudra who was commenting on the holiest of the scriptures. But they could not do anything. Tukaram's fame had reached Shivaji the Great.

Tukaram has written a number of abhangas which are still sung by people. Tukaram wrote about the day to day problems of the people and he was strongly critical of the vices in the people. He preached equality. Tukaram put his signature at the end of every abhanga by using the words "Tuka Mhane" which means "Says Tuka".

Compared to Dnyaneshwara, Tukaram wrote in very simple language. His words are understandable even today. Tukarama's abhanga collection is known as *Gatha* and it is published by the Government of Maharashtra.

Tukaram ended his life at the age of forty two. According to the legends, Lord Vishnu sent His vehicle to collect Tukaram. Tukaram was aware of his end. He has written one abhanga which tells about his departure. It says:

"Amhi jato amuchya gava
Amacha ramram ghyava."

"I am leaving for my abode and I bid goodbye to all of you." The legend says that he went to heaven in his mortal body. In conclusion, nobody knows how he died. He disappeared mysteriously and nobody saw him after that. Some people say that he might have been murdered. Some people say that he went to Pandharpur and lived there anonymously. Some people say that he might have ended his life in Indrayani. Whatever happened, his body was not found.

Tukaram was a very down to earth poet. His words touched people. Only he could write,

"Bhale tari deu kasechi langoti
Nathalache matha hanu kathi."

"We are so soft that when some needy person comes to us we shall part even with our loincloth but if we come across some evil person, we shall break his head."

The pilgrims who make the trip to Pandharpura chant his name along with the earlier saints. They say *"Nivrutti, Dnyandev, Span Muktabai, Eknath Namdev Tukaram"*. And they walk all the way chanting, *"Gnunaba Tuka"*.

Tukaram will always remain alive in the minds of people.

THE PESHWAS

AFTER THE DEATH of the first Bajirao Peshwa, his son Nanasaheb was appointed the Peshwa. Shahu, the Maratha king, trusted him and even though Nanasaheb was ousted once, he was again appointed. He showed his worth by defeating Nizam and also by bringing a lot of money for the Maratha kingdom. In his lifetime Ahmadshah Abdali started attacking and looting the northern region. Nanasaheb sent his cousin Sadashivrao Bhau and son Vishwas to deal with him. In 1761 the Maratha army confronted the Afghan army at Panipat. The Marathas were sandwiched between two armies and they were routed. There were many small kingdoms in the north who remained silent spectators. The Maratha army was massacred. Sadashivrao Bhau disappeared and Vishwasrao died. Nanasaheb got the news and he was so upset that he died within a year. Nanasaheb was a remarkable administrator who gave some discipline to the Maratha Empire. After his death his second son Madhavrao was appointed as Peshwa. This was when the internal conflict in the Peshwa family came to the surface. Nanasaheb's brother Raghunathrao, popularly known as Raghobadada, was ambitious and he started plotting against Madhavrao.

But Madhavrao was a very strong person. He dealt with the internal conflict as well as the external conflict very carefully. He picked up men who were very good and appointed them as his generals. These men became the 12 wise men of the Peshwas. During Madhavrao's times Delhi was controlled by the Marathas. And because of Madhavrao, Marathas recovered from the setback that they had suffered after Panipat's defeat. He defeated the Nijam who always waited for an opportunity to fight back. Madhavrao was a strict person and he had to take stern actions against some of the stalwarts. He had to keep his uncle under house arrest.

But Madhavrao was a sick man. He had TB. The efforts that he took for the re-establishment of the Marathas were too much for him. He died at a young age. Then his brother Narayanrao who was very weak and irresponsible was given the Peshwaship. Raghunathrao, who had kept a low profile during Madhavrao's times now resurged. He and others plotted and executed Narayanrao. After Narayanrao Raghunathrao became the Peshwa. The twelve wise men who controlled the Maratha Raj conspired and ousted Raghunathrao. They appointed a child, Narayanrao's son who was named Sawai Madhavrao and ruled the kingdom for a number of decades.

Raghunathrao remained good for nothing for the rest of his life. He joined the English. There too he started plotting against the wise men of Pune.

The English were not happy with him and finally they handed him over to the Peshwas (according to one account the English recovered all the money spent on Raghunathrao by imposing a special tax on the people).

The last Peshwa to enjoy the prime ministership of the Maratha Empire was Raghunathrao's son Bajirao. He was called Bajirao the second. He did not have any of the qualities of the First Bajirao. Sometimes he sided with the English, sometimes he created trouble, and finally the English defeated him and annexed the Maratha Kingdom to the British Empire. Bajirao was given a yearly pension and was sent to Brahmavart (also known as Bithur).

That was the end of the Peshwa rule. Nana Fadnis with his pen had kept the British away for some twenty five years. It had ended with the death of Sawai Madhavrao.

This Nana had unparalleled cunningness in him. He was related to the Peshwas. In fact his family came to the Maratha empire along with Balaji Vishwanath, the founder of the Peshwa dynasty. Nana had also gone to Panipat along with his wife and mother. After the defeat he could escape, but with a lot of hardships. His wife joined him later but his mother disappeared.

Nana has written an account of his escapade which might be regarded as one of the earliest autobiographies in Marathi. During the times of Madhavrao and later, Sawai Madhavrao quickly rose to key positions. He became a king-maker afterwards.

Nana made Bajirao the Peshwa, but Bajirao had differences with him and he was put in prison. His arrest accelerated the downfall of the Marathas.

Nana is one of the three and a half wise men of the Peshwai period. He was regarded as a 'half' because he was not a warrior like the other wise men, but his pen was very powerful. He kept enemies fighting with each other when the Maratha Empire was in its death throngs. So as a popular saying in Hindi says,

"Nana Nana, Bada sayana
Baki sab janana."

NANASAHEB THE SECOND

THE SECOND BAJIRAO had many wives and he had sons from them but they were short lived. Bajirao adopted a son of one of his dependents, whose name was Dhundiraj and later became known as Dhondopant. He is known to us as Nanasaheb Peshwa.

Bajirao was very fond of him but the British did not approve of the adoption. Bajirao in his will gave all his estate and designations to Nanasaheb. But the British did not accept his will either.

According to his biographers, Nanasaheb was a well read person. He knew Sanskrit, Marathi, Hindostani and also English. He read many newspapers everyday. He also liked to give parties to which he invited the British officers. He had good relations with them but they had very ill opinions about him.

After the death of Bajirao, Nanasaheb applied to the East India Company for his rights which were outright rejected. Nansaheb sent his emissaries to England and one of them tried his level best, but he could not succeed.

Up to 1857, Nanasaheb was loyal to the Company. The Company did not trust him so the officers of the company tried to make life difficult for him. For example, once they encouraged another person from the Peshwa family to claim half the property. Even then Nanasaheb was kind towards them.

The Company had requested him to look after the ammunitions in Kanpur but when he reached Kanpur, the sepoys who had mutinied had reached there. The sepoys requested Nansaheb to lead them. The sepoys made him sit on the throne of Peshwas and there were celebrations.

But the Company was prepared. The battle of Kanpur was won by the sepoys but the next battles were won by the Company. The Company army attacked Bithor and vandalized the Peshwa's palace. Nanasaheb was declared a fugitive and anybody who caught him was promised Rs.One lakh.

Nanasaheb went to Nepal. The exhaustion killed him. Nobody is sure about the end of Nanasaheb.

KHUB LADHI MARDANI VO
TO JHANSI VALI RANI THI
- MAHARANI LAXMIBAISAHEB

MAHARANI LAXMIBAI WAS the daughter of Moropant Tambe, one of the many dependents on Bajirao the Second. She was born in Varanasi, so she was named Mankarnika. They called her Manu. She grew up with Nanasaheb and learnt martial arts with him. She was very bright from the beginning. One legend says that she was not allowed to elephant ride with Nanasaheb because Nanasaheb was a prince and she was a mere daughter of one of Nana's dependents. Manu got very angry and said, "A day will come when I shall have ten such elephants at my doorstep".

Manu was married to Gangadharrao, the king of Jhansi and was named Laxmibai. From a poor Brahmin's daughter she became the queen of Jhansi.

Gangadharrao was a kind person. He was a widower. With the help of the Company he had become the king of Jhansi. He was a good administrator and he had earned respect from the British.

Gangadharrao's first wife had died and he was looking for a suitable bride when he came across Manu. In the course of time Manu gave birth to a child but lost it. Gangadharrao was very sad and he adopted a relative's son who was named Damodarrao.

Gangadharrao died soon afterwards. After his death there were movements from the East India Company to annex the kingdom of Jhansi.

Laxmibai applied to the Company to accept her and give her son the title of Jhansi. The British rejected her application. According to them the adoption was not legal and was not acceptable. Ironically they accepted Damodarrao's claim to the legacy but denied everything to the Queen.

When Laxmibai heard that the British were trying to annex Jhansi, she uttered the famous words, "Meri Jhansi nahi deungi". Rani still had faith in justice and she kept on applying to the high officers of the Company.

Laxmibai was a good administrator and she was respected by the citizens of Jhansi. Godse Bhat had been to Jhansi when Laxmibai was ruling it and he has written an account of his pilgrimage. He saw that she wore the clothes of men and inspected the parade. She sat in the darbar and listened to the grievances and promptly acted on them. According to Godse, she was a beautiful woman. Despite her attire she looked very feminine. Laxmibai had also trained some women who remained with Laxmibai all the time.

The sepoys came to Jhansi and started attacking

the British, Rani did not support them. She might have saved a few lives of the British. The sepoys were leaderless and they were very arrogant. They might have demanded money from the queen.

The residents of Jhansi gave a report of Jhansi in which they targeted Rani. That is how Rani was declared an enemy and a huge army was sent to take care of her. Laxmibai was prepared. The fort of Jhansi was seized but unfortunately the amount was not enough. According to a legend Rani tied her son to her back, rode a horse and jumped from the fort. This is a pure myth because the walls are very high and the horse and the rider both would have died.

The truth is Rani escaped. The British were chasing her. Again she met Godse who has written about this second meeting. Rani told him that she was a widow but for the sake of her nation she had entered this war (the Rani must have said Desh which she must have used for Jhansi, not for the whole of India).

Rani did not give up. She went on fighting although there were none to protect her. The British Officer who fought with her was all praises for her. Finally, she was struck on the head by one soldier. In a wounded state she reached the hut of a sadhu and breathed her last. She told him to cremate her there, so the British could neither defeat her nor capture her after her death.

A popular song says,

"Khub ladhi Mardani Vo To Jhansivali Rani Thi."

TATYA TOPE
(1814 TO 1959)

ATYA WAS ONE general of Marathas who was a big nuisance for the Company's army. For one year they had been trying to catch him, and Tatya covered a distance of thousands of miles during this long chase. The Mutiny ended with Tatya's death.

Tatya was an employee of the last Peshwa. Some scholars think that Tatya was given a very precious cap by the Peshwa, so he was called Tope which means cap. The English historian called him Topi which is the exact word for cap in Marathi. Some people say that he worked with canons in the East India Company. Canon is called Toph in Marathi so it might have been Tope.

Before he joined the Peshwas, he was with many small kingdoms and his specialization was canons or the big guns. Finally, he settled with the Peshwas at Bithor were the Peshwa was kept by the British.

He became a hero after the Sepoy Mutiny. Along with Nanasaheb and Laxmibai he fought with the British and won many battles. Tatya won some and lost some but he was a big menace for the British. His speed was unimaginable.

One day he was at one place and on the second day he was miles away. He became a legend. He had gone to help Laxmibai when Sir Hugh Rose seized Jhansi. Later he fought many battles along with Laxmibai. After Laxmibai's death he fought guerrilla wars. It was very difficult to find him. All of a sudden he would attack and then would vanish again. Tatya had many friends who protected him.

But finally he was caught. He had taken shelter with an employee of the Sindiyas who gave him away. It was by treason that Tatya was caught.

The British generals who saw him on the battlefield were all praise for him.

Tatya was hanged by the British. Some say that the person who was hanged was not Tatya, and that Tatya lived for many more years as a monk.

But the story of Tatya ended with the end of the Sepoy Mutiny.

MAHARAJA RANJIT SINGH

MAHARAJA RANJIT SINGH was the last powerful ruler to establish a big and powerful kingdom. As long as he was alive, the British could not do anything about it. His empire included the whole of Punjab, Kashmir, Sindh, the frontier provinces, and his capital was Lahor.

Ranjit Singh was born to Sikh parents in 1780. His father was a chieftain of a Sikh faction. Ranjit Singh suffered from small pox in his childhood. He lost one eye from it. He had the scars of small pox on his face. But he was a fighter to the core. This did not depress him at all. He became more ambitious after this handicap. He was of short stature like Napoleon and equaled him in military campaigns. After his father's death, Ranjit Singh became the chieftain. He was ambitious so he annexed the small Sikh strongholds to his. While Ahmadshah Abdali's general was passing, his guns were stuck in the Ravi River. Maharaja Ranjit Singh helped him to retrieve the guns so the general rewarded him the title Raja and gifted him the city of Lahor.

Later on Ranjit Singh started calling himself Maharaja Ranjit Singh (there were many Rajas around so he called himself Maharaja).

He checked the Afghans and gave some peace to his citizens. He is regarded as one of the best military strategists. He knew when to attack and when to retreat. In military strategies he was like Shivaji the Great. He had an extraordinary memory. He could remember the revenue of the 10,000 vllages in his kingdom. He also could understand the value of art.

He himself was a devout Sikh but he was not a fanatic. He checked the aggressors but he was not vindictive. People of other religions also worked happily with him. Although blind in one eye he was as able as any other person. His Government was called Khalsa Sarkar. His court was called Khalsa Darbar. For his audiences he liked to be among the people.

Ranjit Singh had his capital in Lahor, which he developed. Even today the signs of Ranjit Singh's rule can be seen there. He had minted coins with the faces of the ten Gurus on them. He was ruling Punjab in the name of the Gurus.

The foreigners who visited Lahor during Ranjit Singh's lifetime have described him in their writing. All agree that Ranjit Singh was a man of extraordinary intelligence.

He had many wives and concubines. He lived a debauched life. He even married girls half his age. The lustful life finally led to ailments. According to

Rajmohan Gandhi's book, once it was even decided to publicly flog him and he had agreed.

The British were watching Ranjit Singh. They wanted a stable Punjab because they were also weary of the Afghans. The Company was also troubled by the Maratha king Yashwantrao Holkar who was an ally of Ranjit Singh.

Ranjit Singh was remarkable in many aspects. We know about his memory. He could also argue on important topics with the learned scholars. His government was clearly a Sikh government and Hindus and Sikhs enjoyed special privileges in his kingdom. Cow slaughter was banned and loud prayers were not allowed for the Muslims. He did not prosecute anybody on account of religion. In fact he wanted to be a king of all Punjabis irrespective of their religion. His closest adviser was a Sufi Muslim.

Ranjit Singh died of paralysis but he was active to the last moment.

VASUDEV BALWANT PHADKE

ASUDEV BALWANT PHADKE raised an army of the Ramoshis and fought with the British. He was finally caught and was sent to Eden where he died. He was unsuccessful in his mission, but his attempt to fight the mightiest empire is unparalleled in the course of India's history. It was one man against an entire force of the British.

Phadke hailed from the Konkan area. He was born in Shirdhon where his memorial stands today. After his primary education he started working in the employment of the British. While he was in Pune, he had an opportunity to listen to Justice Ranade. His speeches organized by Sarvajanik Sabha were eye openers for Phadke. He realized that the misery of the people was the result of the British Governments apathy towards the people of India. There were famines in several parts of the country. He had toured all the areas and he was moved by the plight of the people as well as the animals. The Government was totally indifferent to the woes of the people.

He decided to raise an army and stage an armed revolt. He appealed to all the people but the middle class was not interested in the idea of revolt. It might be because they were used to the carefree life. They enjoyed life in the British Raj and many of them had seen the outcome of the Sepoy Mutiny.

But the nomads responded to his call. He had many men enlisted from the Ramoshi tribe (Ramoshis call themselves the descendents of Rama, the epic Hero). According to some this word is a corrupt form of Ramvanshi which means 'from the clan of Rama'. Ramoshis are fearless and militant. In the earlier system of village administration they were employed as village guards. These people are normaly of well built physique and more than normal height. They are ready to do anything. That was why they were and are called Berads, which is a corrupt form of Bedar (which means one without fear). The shepherd tribe called Dhanagars also enlisted.

Vasudev Balwant himself trained everyone. A later day social reformer Jyotirao Fule had also joined this training centre.

Under the guidance of Vasudev Balwant this army attacked railway stations, post offices, local government quarters called Chawdis and looted them.

Unfortunately these people had no grain of patriotism in them. They only knew how to loot (the British government had listed Ramoshis as criminals). They took the loot and ran away.

Vasudev Balwant was frustrated. He went to the holy places like Ganagapur and later Shri Shailam where he even thought of committing suicide. But then he met one friend who offered all help to him. He promised him that he would get some Rohilas for him (Rohilas are Muslim and they are also known for their militant nature). In the last battle of Panipat they had sided with the Afghans to beat Marathas.

With the help of the Rohilas, Vasudev Balwant again started his attacks. He became a wanted man. According to one account he had sought the blessings of Shri Samarth, who lived at Akkalkot. But that saint indicated to him in gestures that his mission would be unsuccessful.

The British tried their level best to catch him but Vasudev Balwant remained in hiding. When he was tired of his flight, he went to one of the feudal lords of Scindia. He gave him asylum but informed the British. So this nationalist was caught by betrayal. He was tried and given life imprisonment.

Vasudev Balwant tried to escape but was unsuccessful. He refused food because it was of a very low quality and he suffered because of that.

Finally he died in Eden. Actually he killed himself by refusing to take food.

THE EARLY FREEDOM FIGHTERS

ALLEN OCTAVIAN HUME, a retired civil servant and like minded people came together to form the Indian National Congress. The British had learnt something from the revolt and they felt that there should be a platform for the natives to express their grievances or put forth their ideas in a democratic way. The introduction of English education had its effect and a new generation had emerged who looked towards the west as an ideal. The English education had also awakened the educated to the state of our country. Among the first were Dadabhai Navaroji who belonged to the Parsi community, and who was elected to the British Parliament and raised the voice of India there. Dadabhai also worked for women's education. He is called the Bhishma Pitamaha or the grand old man of Indian politics. The next was Justice Ranade who was a scholar and who wrote about the Maratha history. These were the members of the congress and they believed in democratic proceedings. Gopal Krishna Gokhale belonged to the next generation.

Another towering name was Bal Gangadhar Tilak who because of his immence popularity got the name Lokmamya. During their times Congress was divided into two factions. One faction were called moderatists who believed in silent agitations by submitting representations and memos etc. The second faction were called extremists who did not believe in such methods. In both ways the Congress took the demand for freedom to the masses. There were many others who did not believe in peaceful methods. They believed in armed revolution which led to attempts of robbing government treasuries. There were attempts on the lives of British officers. But compared to the peaceful agitations this was on a limited scale.

The early generation of freedom fighters had English education and they believed in peaceful protests and representations. Justice Ranade who was a judge in the British system could manage to do something with his writing. He wrote about the history of the Marathas. There was Gopal Krishna Gokhale who gave a series of talks in England. These were called moderates. Then Tilak came who was called Lokmanya (which literally meant approved by the people). He was aggressive. He ran a newspaper in Marathi and another one in English. His articles and editorials in these papers awakened the people and scared the government. He was tried on charges of sedition in which he himself gave defence. Tilak's contemporary and one time friend Agarkar wanted to bring in social reforms before they went in for political reforms. There were leaders and social reformers in every province. They worked in unity or sometimes alone. The Thakur family (pronounced Tagore by the Western world) had distinguished members like Devendranath, Ravindranath - the first Nobel Laureate from India

The social reformers like Keshavchandra Sen and Jyotirao Phule thought that the British Raj was a Godsend because many good things came to India due to them. The first thing was that education was made available to all irrespective of their caste, colour, and creed. The women could go to schools and colleges. Jyotirao started a school for women. He trained his wife Savitribai as a teacher and she managed the school despite the harassment given to her by the Orthodox people of Pune.

MAHATMA JYOTIRAO PHULE
(1827-1890)

MAHATMA PHULE WAS born to the family of Gorhes who changed their name to Phule because they dealt in flowers. Actually this Gorhe family belonged to the Mali castes who sell flowers.

Jyotirao wanted to learn English and he learnt it despite many difficulties. He could then read English books and also could write something in English. He also had physical training from some masters. He had joined Vasudev Balwant Phadke who trained young people in martial arts. He did not remain with him for long.

Jyotirao was very impressed by what he read. He liked *The Rights of Man* by Thomas Pen. He was fascinated by the American Revolution and their literature. He had made an indepth study of all the Hindu scriptures, and he came to the conclusion that the upper classes had put a number of restrictions on the lower clases to keep them under bondage. According to him the stories woven around the incarnations of Vishnu are the record of the suppression of the lower classes. For example, Waman or dwarf subdued Bali, the mighty king of the Asuras. Jyotirao felt that Bali represented the lower class of the society. He was a very just and righteous man who was envied by the Brahmins of the day, so he was subdued by deception. He was not opposed to Brahmins but he was against the attitude called Brahminism. In fact he was supported by some Brahmins also.

He made available his well to the backward class people who were denied drinking water from the wells of the upper caste people. He started a school for the backward class people. All the rituals were done by the Brahmins, so he trained people to conduct the rituals so that the monopoly of the upper class could be finished.

According to Iravati Karve, Phule did pioneering work in the field of women's education. Her comment is important because her father-in-law Dhondo Keshav Karve is supposed to be the pioneer. He started a school for women and was all for remarriages of the widows. His school for women later became the first women's university in India. Iravati gave this statement because her father-in-law, though a great person, cared only for the Brahmin women. He had no sympathies for women of other castes (another social reformer, Vittal Ramji Shinde, has confirmed this because he had gone to Karve's institute, to get his sister admitted but she could not get admission there).

Phule stands taller than any other reformer because of many things. The educational front was his major feat. In those days the Brahmin girls were married at an early age. Sometimes their husbands died and they became widows at an early age. According to the prevalent customs, they could not remarry. Their heads were tonsured to make them ugly. Phule felt pity for these young widows. He organized a strike of the barbers, who declared that they would not do such a ghastly thing. Many widows strayed or were sometimes unwillingly subjected to sexual exploitations. They became pregnant and to save face resorted to secret ways of abortion. Phule started a home for such ladies. A board on his house said that any woman who had gone astray need not go to the bogus doctors or country medical practitioners. He asked them to come to his place where they would be helped in their deliveries and even their children would be taken care of. He not only preached reform but he practiced it. He had no issues so he adopted one Brahmin boy and gave him his name.

The orthodox hired contract killers to finish Jyotirao but when the killers approached Jyotirao, they were so impressed by his simplicity and sincerity that they gave up their job and became Jyotirao's disciples. Voluntarily, they worked as Jyotiba's bodyguards.

Jyotirao is fondly called Jyotiba. Later on people started calling him Mahatma which means a great soul. This was the title that was given to Gandhiji afterwarwards.

Jyotirao was a self made man. He knew Marathi, Hindi, Sanskrit and English. He could write in any of these languages. He lived a simple life. For a living he took contracts. He did not make much money but whatever he earned went into social work.

When the Prince of Wales came to India, Jyotiba went to see him. He was in the attire of a common man. He said that he represented the common man and he had to be like them only. Jyotirao and his wife were indeed great souls.

He might have taken an extreme stand, he might have interpreted the classics wrongly, but he was the most sincere man of his times who cared for the masses.

That was why Dr. Babasaheb Ambedkar regarded him as his Guru.

DR. BABASAHEB AMBEDKAR
(1891-1956)

DR. BHIMRAO AMBEDKAR was born to Subhedar Ramji and Bhima. Subhedar Ramaji was a well read man who was a follower of the Kabir Pantha. Subhedar was a great influence on Bhimrao. He had his education in Elphinston scool and college. After that he went to Columbia University on a Badoda scholarship where he got his M.A. and Ph.D. in Economics. After returning he had to work in Badoda as an officer for some time.

Right from his childhood days Bhimrao had been experiencing the unjust treatment given to the backward caste people by the upper caste Hindus. All the backward caste people were Shudras in the four tier system of Hindu society. Of the Shudras, some were called Asprushyas, meaning untouchables. Even if by mistake, some untouchable touched some higher caste person, he defiled him and he had to take a bath. The offender was punished. Bhimrao has written that he could not sit with his fellow students but had to sit outside the class. The teachers corrected his notebooks from a distance.

But he was an educated man with a Ph.D. in Economics and he was an officer of the Badoda state. He had to go through humiliating experiences when he was in Badoda. The files were kept on his table after maintaining safe distance.

He left the job and started working for the scheduled castes. He worked in Sydneham College in Mumbai.

His first organization was the Scheduled Caste Federation. He called a convention of the Scheduled Caste people. He implored them to give up the dirty work. The backward castes were given all the dirty work, like sweeping the village or town, taking care of the dead animals etc. For that they were given some land. This was called Gavki. They were given the impression that they were landlords. Dr. Ambedkar requested the people to give up the dirty work and the compensatory land also. He asked them to seek education. Phule had told the people that the plight of the Shudras was because of their apathy towards education. This convention was presided by Shahu Maharaj of Kolhapur who was a descendent of Shivaji the great and had done some pioneering work for the upliftment of the downtrodden.

This started the career of Dr. Babasaheb Ambedkar as the Messiah of the downtrodden.

Shahu Maharaj helped him to go London. He finished his D.Sc. and also became a barrister. After coming back, he worked as a professor and principal of the law colleges and also practiced as a lawyer.

Bahishkrit Hitkarini Sabha was started by him in 1924. He believed all the problems of the backward caste people were rooted in a book called *Manusmruti*. This is a book of laws written by Manu. He publicly burnt this book. The Dalits were not allowed to take drinking water from the reservoir in the village. He staged a Satyagraha in Mahad where there was a pond called Chavdar Tale. He was lathi-charged on this occasion. His next agitation was in Nasik, a holy place. The backward caste people were not given entry in the temples. He wanted entry. The agitation went on for many days. Finally the Kala Ram temple was opened to all castes.

Dr. Ambedkar also participated in the Round Table Conference as a representative of depressed classes. He got separate constituencies for the backward classes sanctioned. Mahatma Gandhi who was also doing something for the backward classes did not like this. He was in jail. He started his indefinite fast to get these separate constituencies cancelled. Finally Dr. Ambedkar had to give in. This is known as the Poona Pact between Mahatma Gandhi and Dr. Babasaheb Ambedkar. According to Dr. Ambedkar this was a stab in the back.

He started All India Scheduled Caste Federation in 1942. When the country was in the grip of the Quit India Movement, Dr. Ambedkar was busy in his activities for the scheduled castes. People like Arun Shourie have written on this. When the whole of India was shouting,

"Simon go back", Dr. Ambedkar met Simon and told him the woes of the backward caste people.

Dr. Babasaheb also worked in the British Government of India. He was the minister of labour.

He founded the People's Education Society, Siddharth College in Mumbai and Milind College of Aurangabad.

He was a voracious reader and he had a collection of 25,000 books. He also wrote a lot. He used to say that he wouldn't be able to live without books. Fortunately his sight was good to the very end.

He wrote a number of books and many articles. *Who were the Shudras*?, *The Annihilation of Caste*, *Buddha and His Dhamma* are some of his well known books.

He was so disturbed by the plight of the scheduled castes that he actually wept when he talked about them. He said, "I was born a Hindu but I shall not die a Hindu."

In Independent India Dr. Babasaheb was a law minister in Pt. Nehru's cabinet. He had differences with Nehru and he resigned.

He was in the drafting committee of India's constitution. That is why he is often referred to as "The Architect of India's constitution". He took great pains to prepare the Hindu Code Bill.

He embraced Buddhism in 1956 along with his followers in Nagpur. The place has now become a pilgrimage spot. He studied all the religions and took this move.

He passed away in the same year. The down trodden lost their father in his death.

He had awakened the down trodden and made them aware of their sorry state, and their plight. He only thought about them. He regarded Kabir and Mahatma Phule as his Gurus. He wanted equality. He tried to get it within the Hindu fold, but when he saw that he just could not bring any change in the upper caste mentality, he decided to change the religion. He chose Buddhism because he felt that Buddism treats all as equal (he was approached by Christians, Muslims and Sikhs also).

If the definition of Brahmin is one who spends his time in learning and teaching, Dr. Ambedkar was a Brahmin par excellence. Unfortunately his own people could not understand him. He contested for Loksabha twice but both the times he lost. He could not get the votes of his own brethren.

That did not stop him. He worked like a karmayogi. He wanted to bring all Shudras under one wing but he was not successful in that. He wanted to form a Republican Party as a forum of the backward caste people. It came into existence after his death.

Today Dr. Ambedkar has become an icon. His followers have deified him.

This would make him very sad.

SHRI RAMKRISHNA
(1836-1886) AND HIS DISCIPLES

SHRI RAMKRISHNA WAS a phenomenon. This man, born in a poor Brahmin family of Begal, had tremendous influence on mankind. A Nobel laureate, Roma Rola, studied his life and wrote his biography for the western world. This simple illiterate man could change the lives of highly educated men like Vivekananda. One who never went to any school, attracted scholars with his simple language and Jesus like parables. They sat at his feet and learnt from him.

Shri Ramkrishna was known as Gadadhar in his early life. He used to have mystic experiences right from his childhood days. The turning point in his life came when he was appointed as a priest in the Kali temple built by Rani Rasmani, a rich and inflencial fisher-woman. Shri Ramkrishna worshipped Mother Kali as if she was a living person. He was very intense in his worshipping. He used do it for hours and he used to cry and speak with the Goddess. Soon people came to know about his extra ordinary pooja of the Goddess. Some regarded him as a lunatic.

Two people came to Ramkrishna to train him in his spiritual journey. One was Totapuri. He was learned in Yoga. After his training, Ramkrishna had experiences of the highest kind. What surprised Totapuri was that Ramkrishna entered into Samadhi. According to him this takes lives to attain, but Ramkrishna attained it within no time. The second person was an elderly Brahmin woman whose name was Bhairavi. She trained Ramkrishna in various forms of worship. According to Bhakti tradition you can worship God in many ways. For example, Hanuman was a very devoted servant of Rama. You can worship Rama like Hanuman. Meera loved Shri Krishna as her beloved. You can worship Krishna like her. You can treat God as a child also. Shri Ramkrishna went through all these different kinds of worship. He attained perfection in each. Then he tried to reach God by different ways like Christianity and Islam. For that he became a Christian and a Muslim.

It was Totapuri who gave the name Ramkrishna to him. After that it was Bharavi Brahmani who proved in an assembly of learned people that Shri Ramkrishna was an incarnation of God or a prophet on mission.

After that Ramkrishna's fame spread everywhere. It was Shri Keshabchandra Sen a social reformer and founder of the Brahmo Samaj who became an ardent devotee. Maharshi Devendranath Thakor also used to come to Shri Ramkrishna but he was awaiting the arrival of his young disciples.

They came in the last phase of his life. There were some married men and there were some young boys. They became his disciples and spread his word throughout the world.

He taught them that all religions are true. Every doctrinal system represents a path to God. He had followed every path and had come to that conclusion. He also experienced that the different ideologies represent the different stages in man's life. Dualism or Dwaita is true and Adwaita is also true.

During his last days, he suffered from cancer. He had severe pains but he never demanded anything from the Goddess. This was Christ-like and endured all the pains of Crucifixion. The similarity does not end there. He talked in simple language like Christ did and also spoke in parables.

He trained Swami Vivekananada and many other young people who were of equal caliber. The monks who later got the names Swami Brahmananda, Saradananda, Premananda, Akhandananda, Turiyananda Adbhutananda, Ramkrishnananda etc., were all of the same age and had all come from good Bengali backgrounds, were trained by Shri Ramkrishna and later by his wife Shri Saradadevi and Swami Vivekananda.

Shri Ramkrishna's wife Shri Sarada Devi was an equally great person. For this extra ordinary couple the whole world was a family. She too was illiterate. She was led on the spiritual path by Shri Ramkrishna himself. She learnt whatever was taught to her by Shri Ramkrishna. There was something innate in her.

She was a mother and she looked after all the monastic and household devotees of the master as her children. They too regarded her as mother and always took her opinion in every matter. She used to say, "My son, none is a stranger in this world. All are one".

The most notable disciple of Shri Ramkrishna was Swami Vivekananda. He was known as Narendra in his earlier avatar. Naren was the son of a successful Calcutta lawyer. He was very naughty and inquisitive from the very beginning. His grasping of any subject was beyond anybody's comprehension. He could read tomes within hours and had a gifted memory. He was interested in theology but he could not get the answers to the questions in his mind. He had written a letter to Herbert Spencer after reading his book. He used to go to the meetings of Brahmo where he saw Shri Ramkrishna once. He thought of him as a mad person.

Once his English professor came across the word trance while teaching one of William Wordsworth's poem. Trance is a semiconscious state which is experienced by mystics. The mystics enjoy divine joy or blissful state when they are in trance. The professor said that he knew one person who remained in trance state for a long time.

He said that it was the priest at the Kali temple; Shri Ramkrishna. Naren went to see him. The first meeting changed the couse of Naren's life. Shri Ramkrishna touched him and he experienced that blissful state of Samadhi.

After that Naren went regularly to see Ramkrishna. A person like him, with keen intellect and immense reading, found that there was a lot for Shri Ramkrishna to give him. Ramkrishna had that gift. It had come to him through his intense sadhana (spiritual practices). A whole new world of ancient knowledge opened before Naren. Ramkrishna trained him in a systematic way. Earlier Naren did not believe in idol worshipping but Ramkrishna made him see the sense of it.

Before his passing away Shri Ramkrishna initiated all those young boys into sanyasa (renunciation). He wanted Naren to lead them. After Shri Ramkrishna's passing away, they bought an old building and started living like monks.

The next phase in Naren's life was marked by his touring the whole of India. He saw the poverty, the illiteracy, the plight of the backward caste, and women. He saw that the common man was in the throngs of all these. He wanted to change that but still he did not know what could be done.Wherever he went, people were impressed by his personality, his knowledge, and his love for the motherland.

He had many disciples. The kings and princes of the states of India were very impressed by his ideas. During these times he took different names and finally settled on Vivekananda.

His biographers write that when he arrived at Kanyakumari, he swam to the rock and meditated on that for some time and during this meditation, he was enlightened like Buddha. His couse of action was finalized in his mind. Shri Rramkrishna's teaching and the knowledge that he had gained during his travelling gave him his ideals.

A convention of all religious faiths was organized in Chicago. It was called the "Parliament of Religion". Scholars representing different faiths were invited and Swamiji's disciples decided that he would go to America to represent ancient Indian faith.

All of them collected money to send Swamiji to America. A passage on a ship was booked and Swamiji went to America. He reached America. He had no proper clothes to wear and he had literally no money. On top of that when he reached the office of the organizers he came to know the deadline for enrolement was over and he could not be given entry.

He was going back, but on the train he met a passenger who was very impressed with his knowledge. He had a lot of influence. He gave a recommendation letter and Swamiji could get entry. The organizers told him that he could talk only for three minutes at the end of the session. When he rose to speak, he greeted the gathering with "My dear sisters and brothers of America"; the audience was stunned for a moment and after that applauded for several minutes. The speech itself was very effective. He told them that all roads lead to one and the same God. For next day's newspapers this was the breaking news. An Indian monk had conquered America. Swamiji told them about India and about India's heritage and Indians and Swamiji was the most sought out speaker in that parliament of religions.

That was the beginning of the phenomenal Vivekananda. Swamiji was invited at different places to deliver his talks. There was a fee charged.

When he returned to India, he was given a hero's welcome. Then he founded the Ramkrishna Mission which according to him was an organization of selfless workers. Once in India he was very critical of his fellow citizens. He lashed them about their illiteracy, superstitions and everything else that was blocking their progress. He gave them the true meaning of Dharma. Whenever there was any calamity he rushed there with his disciples. His work was lauded even by the government of India.

Swamiji passed away at the age of 39. He remained active and young to his last breath. His birthday and that week is called youth week.

Swamiji awakened India. He rejuvenated the Sanatana Dharma. Because of him the Western world came to know that India was not a pagan country. He convinced the Americans that we in India did not need any religion or philosophy but we needed bread.

His efforts might have accelerated the process of freedom which we got in 1947. There is a renewed interest in the teachings of Swami Vivekananda. His disciples have written his biography in two volumes and his lectures; letters have been compiled and published under the title, *The Collected Works of Swami Vivekananda*. As a book he wrote only one book titled *Rajyoga* but he has talked and given discourses on almost every subject. He was a monk but he did not belive in living a secluded life. Shri Ramkrishna had told him that God resides in every human being so serving the masses was equal to serving the God. He was against conventions. He wanted India to learn something from the West and march towards progress. Because of his revolutionary thoughts he was called the Warrior Monk. The description fitted him.

He achieved a lot within his lifespan of thirty nine years. The organization that he built, the Ramkrishna Mission, is flourishing and has been doing all the work that he had told the monks to do.

These two, Shri Ramkrishna and Swamiji are unparalled in the history of Modern India.

MAHATMA GANDHI

THE BOOK ON India's glorious past cannot be complete without mentioning Mahatma Gandhi, the father of the nation. This simple man wearing only a loin cloth shook the foundations of the British Empire. His tactics were simple but very effective. He changed the lives of millions of Indians. It was he who took the Congress movement to the masses. There were leaders before who were trying to awaken India; their success was moderate. Gandhiji did not believe in violence. He did not believe in violent methods. He coined a few new terms. One was Satyagraha which means insistence on truth. The second was Ahimsa which means non-violence. The third term was Asahakar which means non-cooperation. The mighty British Empire was stunned by these weapons.

Mohandas Karamchand Gandhi was born in Porbandar in Gujarat. His father was the diwan of the state. According to his autobiography he had many vices in his childhood. But one instance changed him. He was married to Kasturba. After his preliminary education he went to England to get his barrister's degree. He came back but could not do anything for a while. Then one Indian merchant who had business in South Africa invited him. Gandhiji experienced the racist nature of the white people. He was thrown out of a railway compartment even though he had a full reservation because he could not travel with the white-skinned people. Gandhiji saw that any person who was not white was called 'coolie' by the whites and was treated very contemptuously.

Gandhiji was the first to raise his voice against the Rowlette Act which required every non white person to carry an identity card. He united all non whites and publicly burned those identity cards. This was the beginning of Mahatma Gandhi. In South Africa he was impressed by a book titled *Unto the Last* by John Ruskin. He tried to implement this philosophy. He bought one farm and lived there with his family. Everything they needed was grown in this farm. Everybody had to work. He named the farm after Count Lev Tolstoy (the farm is still there in South Africa). Gandhiji's rules were very strict and nobody was exempt from these rules.

Gandhiji won his battle partially in South Africa (the racial discrimination was to continue for another hundred years).

Gandhiji came back to India and decided to join the freedom movement. By now his fame had reached India. He met Gopal Krishna Gokhale, who he regarded as his political Guru. Gokhale told him to tour the whole of India to know the country and the countrymen.

Gandhiji travelled by third class where he could meet the real India. He was moved by the poverty and the suffering of the real India. While he was in Africa he had given up western dress. After watching the poverty, he gave up wearing full dress. He decided that he would remain only in a loin cloth which was all the poor of India could afford. He remained like that to the end of his life.

His first clash with the British Empire was at Champaran where the Indigo workers were exploited by the British. After the death of Lokmanya Tilak, the helms of Indian National Congress came into Gandhiji's hands.

Gandhiji was very simple. He understood the pulse of India. Armed struggle was not for the masses. He gave new weapons to fellow Indians. He lived in a small hut and took pure vegetarian food.

The weapon of Satyagraha was very powerful. Under Gandhiji's guidance, people of India used this weapon against the British Empire. One has to see the clips to believe in the power of it. The volunteers marched with banners in their hand. They protested; armed police charged on them but the volunteers did not resist. They were wounded, they fell down. The women volunteers took them away. They were nursed and bandaged. Again these volunteers came forward to take the beating of the British police.

When British government imposed tax on salt, Gandhiji declared that he would make salt and defy the law. Gandhiji's march started from a place called Dandi. This is known as the Dandi March and salt Satyagraha. The whole of India took part in it.

Gandhiji changed the lives of Indians. He told people to give up their jobs, schools and join the freedom movement.

He appealed to them to not use foreign made items. There was burning of foreign made things like clothes all over India. People like Jawaharlal Nehru gave up everything and joined the freedom movement. Nehru's father Motilal had a roaring practice as a lawyer. He started living in the way Gandhiji had told him to. This is one example, but there were many who left colleges, and jobs to join the freedom movement. People underwent torture and death but they remained firmly adhered to Gandhiji's principles.

The Pathans of Frontier province are militants. Khan Abdul Gafar Khan worked amongst them and united them under the banner; "Khudai Kidmadgar". The militants were talking non-violence and non-resistance. This was close to a miracle and this was the result of Gandhiji's teaching.

Gandhiji observed fast once a week. He also used it as a weapon. Whenever he was unhappy over something, whenever he wanted something done, he declared 'fast unto death'.

In 1942 he started Chale Jav or Quit India Movement. He told the British to quit India. In 1947, India became independent at the cost of a partition. Two nations, India and Pakistan, came into existence. It was on the base of religion. Gandhiji tried his level best but he was helpless. He regarded himself as the leader of both Hindus and Muslims, but the Muslims did not accept him and the Hindus had become contemptuous of him.

When India was celebrating freedom, this man, who was called the father of the nation, was amongst the people who were the victims of the Hindu Muslim riots. He had lost his appetite for living. Earlier he used to say that he would live up to a hundred and twenty five years, but after the partition, the trainful of dead bodies (which he was forced to watch), this man who had challenged and defeated the mighty empire felt that he was defeated by his own sons. He yearned for death.

A very cruel death awaited him. On 30th Jan 1948, Nathuram Godse shot him when he was going to a prayer meeting. Gandhiji who was feeling old and had lost the appetite for living, died instantly.

Godse was caught and many others who were involved in the conspiracy were caught and they were tried. Veer Savarkar was also arrested and tried but the court aquitted him. That involvement finished him politically.

Godse and Apte, the main culprits were hanged. The rest of them were given life sentences. Savarkar was exonerated.

But did Gandhiji die on that day? No, he didn't. He went on living in the hearts of millions. He still continues to influence us. Recently there was a Hindi movie, "*Lage Raho Munnabhai*" which was based on Gandhian Philosophy. When South Africa became independent, they too remembered Ganhiji.

216

www.ingramcontent.com/pod-product-compliance
Lightning Source LLC
Chambersburg PA
CBHW031251090426
42742CB00007B/410